Project AIR FORCE

SERVICE RESPONSES TO THE EMERGENCE OF JOINT DECISIONMAKING

Leslie Lewis
Roger Allen Brown
C. Robert Roll

Prepared for the
UNITED STATES AIR FORCE

RAND

The research reported here was sponsored by the United States Air Force under Contract F49642-01-C-0003. Further information may be obtained from the Stategic Planning Division, Directorate of Plans, Hq USAF.

Library of Congress Cataloging-in-Publication Data

Lewis, Leslie.
    Service responses to the emergence of joint decisionmaking / Leslie Lewis,
Roger Allen Brown, C. Robert Roll.
        p. cm.
    MR-1438
    Includes bibliographical references.
    ISBN 0-8330-3069-8
    1. United States—Armed Forces—Decision making. 2. United States. Dept. of
Defense—Decision making. I. Brown, Roger Allen, 1940– II. Roll,
Charles Robert. III. Title.

UA23 .L525 2001
355.3'3041—dc21

                                                                    2001048555

RAND is a nonprofit institution that helps improve policy and decisionmaking through research and analysis. RAND® is a registered trademark. RAND's publications do not necessarily reflect the opinions or policies of its research sponsors.

Published 2001 by RAND
1700 Main Street, P.O. Box 2138, Santa Monica, CA 90407-2138
1200 South Hayes Street, Arlington, VA 22202-5050
201 North Craig Street, Suite 102, Pittsburgh, PA 15213-1516
RAND URL: http://www.rand.org/
To order RAND documents or to obtain additional information,
contact Distribution Services: Telephone: (310) 451-7002;
Fax: (310) 451-6915; Email: order@rand.org

The Department of Defense's (DoD's) decisionmaking processes have changed since the passage of the Goldwater-Nichols legislation in 1986 and the collapse of the Soviet Union in 1989. While some members of DoD would argue that there has been substantial change, others would argue that these changes are marginal at best. Since the early 1960s, the Planning, Programming, and Budgeting System (PPBS) has been DoD's key decisionmaking process. The enactment of the Goldwater-Nichols legislation (the Goldwater-Nichols Department of Defense Reorganization Act of 1986) introduced new players and changed fundamental relationships among many of the old players. The Chairman of the Joint Chiefs of Staff (CJCS) was empowered to provide independent advice to the Secretary of Defense and to the President. The Services were no longer solely responsible for defining requirements; they now had to be responsive to the commanders in chief (CINCs).

These changes in the resource environment have occurred during a period that saw the collapse of the Soviet Union and the emergence of a multipolar world. The period between 1986 and 2000 was also marked by significant decreases in U.S. defense expenditures concurrent with substantial military deployments.

This report addresses changes in the resource environment since 1986 and the military departments' responses to those changes, describing and assessing how the departments of the Army, Navy, and Air Force have redefined their planning and programming functions. Organizational and functional alignments since the passage of the Goldwater-Nichols legislation are also examined. The research relies on formal and informal documentation and on interviews with members of the various military departments, the Office of the Secretary of Defense (OSD), and the Joint Staff. The cutoff date for this research was December 2000.

This study was sponsored by the Plans and Programs Office (XP) in the Department of the Air Force and was performed within the Resource Management program of Project AIR FORCE.

PROJECT AIR FORCE

Project AIR FORCE, a division of RAND, is the Air Force federally funded research and development center (FFRDC) for studies and analyses. It provides the Air Force with independent analyses of policy alternatives affecting the development, employment, combat readiness, and support of current and future aerospace forces. Research is performed in four programs: Aerospace Force Development; Manpower, Personnel, and Training; Resource Management; and Strategy and Doctrine.

CONTENTS

In fall 1998, the Air Force leadership asked RAND's Project AIR FORCE to assess how the military departments—Army, Navy, and Air Force—conduct their planning and programming functions. The Air Force wanted to know what decision models each Service uses for planning and programming. In particular, the client wanted to know how the decision models have changed since the passage of the Goldwater-Nichols Department of Defense Reorganization Act of 1986. Among the issues the Air Force wanted the assessment to address were the following:

1. How have the Goldwater-Nichols legislation and the collapse of the Soviet Union affected decisionmaking within DoD?

2. Why are the acquisition function and the associated decisionmaking processes disconnected from the PPBS?

3. How have the other Services responded to the changes brought about by the passage of the Goldwater-Nichols legislation?

4. How might the Air Force improve its planning and programming and the supporting decisionmaking processes?

This assessment focuses on the decisionmaking processes within DoD and how the military departments interact with them. The evaluation discusses the "ideal" systems and how the systems are designed to operate as well as how the systems are actually working.

The study builds on prior RAND studies of decisionmaking. The research team also interviewed individuals from the Army, Navy, Air Force, and the Joint Staff and OSD about how requirements, PPBS, and acquisition processes function and about their expectations regarding what the processes produced. The team examined both formal and informational documentation.

The analytic template for the assessment is the simple economic model of supply, demand, and integration. Other RAND work has used this template to evaluate the effectiveness of processes and decisionmaking in large, complex bureaucracies, such as DoD.

The PPBS is DoD's primary system for examining the planning, allocation, and management of defense resources. It links the overall national security strategy to specific programs. The PPBS was designed to facilitate fiscally constrained planning, programming, and budgeting in terms of complete programs—forces and systems—rather than through artificial budget categories. As such, it is one of the Secretary of Defense's key management tools, providing the means to set and control the department's agenda.

The acquisition function is subordinate to the PPBS process; it deals with the "how to buy" question after the PPBS process has decided what to buy. Several initiatives have been undertaken in DoD to ensure that the process for acquiring systems is efficient and cost-effective. The most notable was that of the President's Blue Ribbon Commission on Acquisition Reform, better known as the Packard Commission, which published its findings in 1985. The commission's recommendations, which called for fundamental redesign of the acquisition function, were implemented through both the Goldwater-Nichols legislation and the Acquisition Reform Act. The acquisition function was moved to the Service Secretariats and was managed by a civilian. A three-tiered management structure under civilian control was established. Within OSD, an under secretary position was created to manage DoD acquisition and, later, research and technology.

The passage of Goldwater-Nichols changed decisionmaking within DoD by altering the dynamics of the PPBS and acquisition processes. The legislation gave the CINCs a stronger voice in defining operational requirements, as well as the resources necessary to perform their missions. The CINCs' spokesperson is the CJCS. The CJCS and his staff, the Joint Staff, were assigned the responsibility of integrating CINC requirements, setting priorities, and demonstrating how the requirements were related to joint operational readiness.

Goldwater-Nichols directed the military departments to provide the capabilities necessary to meet CINC-defined operational requirements. The Services were specifically directed that their job was to man, train, and equip the forces to be able to respond to CINC operational demands. On the basis of this charter, the Joint Staff's activities have gradually expanded to include many dimensions of planning, programming, and budgeting. The evolutionary process of Joint Staff involvement in the PPBS has resulted in the development of new processes and, in some cases, the redesign of existing processes and forums. The 1991 Gulf War accelerated the direct involvement of the Joint Staff in resourcing because it confirmed to many in Congress and OSD that the Goldwater-Nichols legislation had established the correct decision model. The new processes, with their supporting reports, include the Chairman's Program Recommendations, the Chairman's Program Assessment, the Joint Warfighting Capabilities Assessment, and the expanded Joint Requirements Oversight Council. All contribute to and reflect the expanded responsibilities of the Joint Staff and the CJCS.

In response to these changes in decisionmaking processes and the military departments' perceived challenge to their dominance, the Services have all undergone organizational changes and redesigned their PPBS processes. This reengineering has often resulted in headquarters reorganizations in response to the congressionally directed changes (contained in the Goldwater-Nichols legislation) and because of the Services' belief that some realignment was necessary to improve internal decisionmaking processes.

ARMY

Of the three Services, the Army was the most responsive to the changes the legislation directed. The Army's resource decision model reflects its focus on force structure and end strength, stressing centralized decisionmaking and decentralized execution. The Army headquarters provides the planning and programming guidance to the major commands and operating agencies.

The Deputy Chief of Staff for Operations and Plans (DCSOPS) dominates resource decisionmaking within the Army because, until recently, he owned the force structure–end strength and modernization portfolios. He also sets the priorities for all Army requirements, ensuring that near-term operational demands are met.

In 1995, the Army leadership concluded that the Service's planning and programming functions were not providing sufficient visibility into the totality of Army resources and the development of possible options. One critical point is that, since the Army is a hierarchical decisionmaking institution, the Secretariat wants to ensure that it participates at each critical level rather than only at the highest decisionmaking levels of the institution. In 1995, the Army's goal was to sustain a large force structure and end strength. Its decisionmaking processes did not provide for trade-offs or for a strong institutional debate about what was important over the near, mid-, and long terms.

The Army's reengineering process included functional, process, and organizational change. These changes have been gradually implemented over several program cycles. The process as designed includes reestablishing institutional vision and strategic planning. Rather than relying on the Army's own assessment of the geostrategic environment, the strategic planning process has been refocused on institutional responses to the operational demands the CINCs and the Joint Staff are placing on the Army. In its provider role, the Army develops and fields capabilities to meet CINC demands. Critical to balancing supply and demand is the development of a strong integration function. The integration function develops and assesses resource alternatives to ensure that the Army leadership is fully informed about what alternatives are available and their possible implications for the institution over the near, mid-, and long terms.

An institutional vision and strategic plan drive the Army's process. A healthy tension between operational and institutional demands is adjudicated through the development of options. The goal is to have maximum visibility of the key issues confronting the institution and an understanding of their potential cross-functional impacts. To support this conceptual framework, the Army developed mission areas and six program evaluation groups. The Army mission areas are derived from the CINCs' missions; the institutional demands concentrate on the Title 10 functions: man, equip, and train.

The planning and programming process is supported by a series of hierarchical decisionmaking bodies. All decisionmaking bodies within the Army are cochaired. The hierarchical nature of decisionmaking within the Army attempts to ensure that, at each level, appropriate issues are raised and adjudicated on the basis of leadership guidance.

The Army is attempting to further institutionalize its redesigned planning and programming processes through the realignment of the offices of DCSOPS and the Assistant Vice Chief of Staff of the Army (AVCSA). Late in 2000, the Chief of Staff of the Army directed that the AVCSA office be renamed and realigned. DCSOPS was divested of the modernization portfolio, and responsibility for it moved to AVCSA's office, which was renamed the Deputy Chief of Staff for Programs. The remaining DCSOPS responsibilities were refocused on near-term operational readiness and on prioritizing the total Army requirements. DCSOPS would retain oversight over the strategic planning process, mission area analyses, and force structure. In addition to managing the modernization portfolio, DCSOPS fiscally constrained options that address the requirements' priorities, program development and balance, and analytic support.

NAVY

The focus of Navy planning and programming is long-term investment. In 1992, the Navy headquarters and Secretariat staffs were reorganized in response to criticisms from Congress concerning the Navy's unresponsiveness to Goldwater-Nichols. The Navy's current decisionmaking model stresses centralized decisionmaking and centralized execution. The reorganization eliminated the stovepiped planning and programming functions that had each platform or system commander identifying his own plan and resourcing it.

The Department of the Navy's reengineering activities paid particular attention to the increased involvement of the Joint Staff in resource decisionmaking. The institution organizationally and functionally realigned according to the Joint Staff. Embedded within the structure is the Marine Corps, which sustains a separate PPBS capability.

The Navy's decision model relies on a strong integration function. The Deputy Chief of Naval Operations, N8 (Resources, Requirements, and Assessments), is responsible for development of the program investment plan, for development of fiscally constrained investment options, and for assessment of the Navy's program to ensure that it is balanced. N8 is also responsible for representing the

Navy in all forums and activities related to the development, presentation, and justification of the Navy's program.

The Navy uses a planning and programming assessment framework similar to that of the Joint Staff. The framework is divided into two areas: joint mission areas and support areas. Different organizations within N8 are responsible for conducting the assessments, but the outputs of the assessments form the basis for generating alternatives and investment options. This approach enables the Navy to better explain its investment decisions to the Joint Requirements Oversight Council, the Joint Review Board, and the Defense Resources Board.

Strategic resource planning and programming predominate within the Navy. Institutional planning is done to ensure that the Navy is responsive to the Joint Strategic Planning System and its outputs. This occurs in N3/N5 (Plans, Policy, and Operations). N8 is responsible for resources, requirements, and assessments and is the dominant resource organization within the military department.

The Navy PPBS process is designed around OSD's PPBS schedule. The strategic planning phase is biennial but of shorter duration than those of the Army and Air Force. Strategic resource planning is integral to the program planning phase. The Integrated Warfighting Architecture Review System process examines Navy requirements within the context of what is desired, what currently exists, and what is planned. These analyses provide Navy leadership an objective integrated baseline for current Navy plans and for future requirements.

Both the civilian and military leaderships actively participate in a three-tiered committee process that reviews the various investment options as they emerge through the programming phase. The Secretariat plays a strong role in developing and executing the Service program, independently reviews the program, and provides recommendations to the Chief of Naval Operations. Differences are resolved in the various decisionmaking forums in which the civilian and military leaderships jointly participate. The Navy Program Integration Center provides integration and a baseline for decisionmaking that informs both the military and civilian leaderships of current program decisions.

The Navy's hierarchical and shared decisionmaking structure ensures that all important resource issues are vetted at the appropriate level. The Investment Balance Review process provides a critical mechanism for ensuring that controversial issues within the Navy are discussed and settled prior to any external reviews. Most of the leadership concludes that the Navy's planning, programming, and budgeting structure is responsive to the internal and external demands being placed on the Navy.

In fall 2000, the Navy leadership decided that N8 had become too powerful and that near-, mid-, and long-term readiness issues were of sufficient magnitude to warrant addressing them both organizationally and functionally. The Navy also determined that its highly centralized decision model frequently excluded close examination and resourcing of the fleet. The objective of the realignment is to ensure that requirements and programs receive the appropriate attention and that a healthy tension exists among requirements and resources. A reinvigorated N7 (Warfare Requirements and Programs) would now be the advocate for requirements and programs. N8 would be responsible for overseeing resources and developing fiscally constrained options that address the totality of Navy resources. In addition, the Office of the Deputy Chief of Naval Operations, N4 (Fleet Readiness and Logistics), was reorganized to become a single advocate for fleet readiness issues.

AIR FORCE

The focus of Air Force decisionmaking is on investment in modernization and basing. The Air Force model for decisionmaking is consensus-built, centralized decisionmaking and decentralized execution. The Air Force underwent two significant organizational reform efforts to reach this decision model, one in 1989 and the other in 1992. The preponderance of Air Force efforts during the 1989 reorganization was on the realignment of the acquisition and logistics functions. In the course of this reorganization, the Air Force leadership concluded that authority and responsibility should be assigned at the lowest "reasonable" level. In response to this philosophy, Air Staff functions were pushed to the major commands (MAJCOMs). In 1989, for example, the integration function was substantially weakened, while the demand and supply functions were strengthened. The roles of the MAJCOMs were altered to involve them directly in the Air Force planning and programming functions. The ability of the acquisition function to define future requirements and to provide systems was strengthened through centralizing power in the Service Acquisition Executive for all system acquisition and through direct involvement in requirements generation and validation.

The 1992 reorganization reinforced this model by abolishing the three-star programmer position and replacing it with a two-star position that was not empowered to generate independent options. The critical planning and programming functions were sent to the MAJCOMs. The major role of the programmer was now to assess issues raised by the Secretary of the Air Force (SAF) and the Chief of Staff of the Air Force (CSAF), because they were the integrators of information from the MAJCOMs.

The decentralized planning and programming function hindered the Air Force's overall ability to effectively generate alternative program options, particularly in a period in which defense expenditure was declining. As a partial remedy to this problem, CSAF reestablished the council–corporate board structure in 1996 to provide some capability to adjudicate issues within a broader participatory body. The board structure was organized around missions and mission support functions. Although its goal was to facilitate improvements in Air Force planning and programming, the board structure addressed issues only through the missions and mission support function stovepipes. Thus, there was no visibility into how the MAJCOMs and the panels made decisions.

To address this problem partially, the then-CSAF established a single Air Staff organization to handle the corporate planning and programming function. The goal was to establish an integrated planning and programming capability at the corporate level that could link Air Force planning and programming efforts and assist the Air Force in proactively shaping joint and OSD planning and resource activities. This reorganization did not, however, address MAJCOM planning and programming activities and did not change the corporate-board structure.

Continued dissatisfaction with the Air Force's planning and programming activities, combined with congressionally mandated reductions in the headquarters staffs of all the Services, has led to the Headquarters Air Force 2002 (HAF02) initiative. This initiative, which the SAF and the CSAF are sponsoring, focuses on process reengineering and organizational realignments that are designed to address some of the problems identified above. The HAF02 activity is examining such areas as requirements development and approval, administrative support functions, the mission planning process, and the roles of the MAJCOMs vis-à-vis the Air Staff. Its desired outputs are improved internal and external process alignments, streamlined decisionmaking processes, and staff efficiencies. As with every large reengineering effort, however, this one has bogged down. The baselining activities were completed late in 2000, but no organizational or functional realignments have yet occurred. In fall 2000, the Air Force leadership decided to initiate an experiment, the objective of which is to further empower the MAJCOMs by allocating top lines and budgets to them. The role of the headquarters is to review the MAJCOM programs for balance and risk. As of this writing, the experiment is still under way.

CONCLUSIONS AND RECOMMENDATIONS

The involvement of the Joint Staff in resource decisionmaking has far exceeded what the designers of the Goldwater-Nichols legislation had envisioned. In part, this has been in response to change in the geostrategic environment brought about by the collapse of the Soviet Union. Goldwater-Nichols was designed to counterbalance the dominance of the Services in the determination of forces and weaponry with that of the CJCS and the CINCs.

Neither OSD nor the Joint Staff has yet fully resolved where the other's functional responsibilities rest. The 1996–1997 Quadrennial Defense Review revealed that the two organizations have substantially different perspectives. The disunity of the Joint Staff and OSD provides opportunities for the Services to influence all aspects of DoD decisionmaking. In doing so, however, the military departments must be keenly attuned to all aspects of OSD and Joint Staff activities that could affect them. It also necessitates that the Services have well-defined planning, programming, and budgeting functions.

In the end, there is no perfect decision model. The models the services use reflect their respective institutional cultures. The Army's centralized decisionmaking–decentralized execution model reflects an emphasis on retaining force structure and end strength. The Navy's highly centralized model reflects a focus on investment. The Air Force's highly decentralized model grew out of a failure to fully understand the ramifications of the 1989 and 1992 reorganizations. The leadership's goal was to establish a centralized decisionmaking–decentralized execution model. For such a model to work, however, CSAF and SAF must vigorously participate in all aspects of Air Force decisionmaking as the key decisionmakers, as well as the integrators and developers of options. Yet the model's implementation was far too personality-dependent for subsequent CSAFs and SAFs to adhere to it, particularly in light of the increased complexities in DoD's processes since the early 1990s.

All the Services have undertaken reengineering initiatives since the passage of Goldwater-Nichols. The most recent are those of the Army and the Air Force. As of this writing, both Services' initiatives are focused on addressing the increased demands of the Joint Staff's processes and enhancing their ability to interact successfully with OSD and CJCS. This research suggests that the Services have come to realize that they not only need to be responsive to the external processes that define and allocate their resources but must also be able to use these processes to advocate their perspectives and achieve the desired resource outcomes.

ACKNOWLEDGMENTS

This work was supported by a number of individuals within RAND. Natalie Crawford, Vice President of Project AIR FORCE, supported the analyses and involved the researchers in a variety of issues concerning Air Force decisionmaking and the supporting processes. Katharine Webb provided data and shared insights on OSD planning and programming. Earlier work done by Carl Builder on Service cultures provided a foundation for understanding the evolution of Service decisionmaking processes.

Members from the different Services, the Joint Staff, and OSD provided data and held long discussions with the project team on various aspects of their resource decision processes and on the processes' strengths and weaknesses. We cannot acknowledge them all, but we are thankful for their support.

Research assistants Kenneth Myers, Anissa Thompson, and Traci Williams supported the project by gathering research data, researching prior reorganizations, and organizing the project's voluminous papers. Danielle Johnson Zink integrated changes, and Deanna Weber formatted the final document.

Finally, the project team would like to thank Dr. Clark Murdock, former Deputy Director of Air Force Strategic Planning (XPX). His insights and comments on various aspects of the work as it evolved were extremely helpful.

ABBREVIATIONS

ABO	Army Budget Office
ACAT	Acquisition category
ACC	Air Combat Command
ACTD	Advanced concept technology demonstration
ADCSOPS	Assistant Deputy Chief of Staff for Operations [Army]
AETC	Air Force Education and Training Command
AFAE	Air Force Senior Acquisition Executive
AFLC	Air Force Logistics Command
AFMC	Air Force Materiel Command
AFRAP	Air Force Resource Allocation Process
AFSC	Air Force Systems Command
APOM	Air Force Program Objectives Memorandum
APPG	Air Force Planning and Programming Guidance
ARA	Acquisition Reform Act
ARSTAF	Army staff
ASA(FM&C)	Assistant Secretary of the Army for Financial Management and Comptroller
ASA(I&E)	Assistant Secretary of the Army for Installations and Environment

ASD(PA&E)	Assistant Secretary of Defense for Program Analysis and Evaluation
ASPG	Army Strategic Planning Guidance
AVCSA	Assistant Vice Chief of Staff, Army
C^4	Command, control, communications, and computers
CINC	Commander in chief
CJCS	Chairman of the Joint Chiefs of Staff
CNO	Chief of Naval Operations
CPR	Chairman's Program Recommendations
CSA	Chief of Staff, Army
CSAF	Chief of Staff, Air Force
DAB	Defense Acquisition Board
DAMO	Department of the Army Management Office
DAMO-FD	DAMO–Force Development
DAMO-OD	DAMO–Operations and Readiness
DAMO-SS	DAMO–Strategy
DAMO-ZR	DAMO–Resource Analysis and Integration
DC	Dynamic Commitment
DCSOPS	Deputy Chief of Staff for Operations and Plans [Army]
DCSPRO	Deputy Chief of Staff for Programs [Army]
DEPSECDEF	Deputy Secretary of Defense
DMR	Directed Management Review
DoD	Department of Defense
DON	Department of the Navy
DONPIC	Department of Navy Program Integration Center
DPA&E	Director of Program Analysis and Evaluation

DPAB	Defense Planning Advisory Board
DPG	Defense Planning Guidance
DRB	Defense Resources Board
ES	End strength
FOA	Field Operating Agency
FS	Force structure
FY	Fiscal year
FYDP	Future Years Defense Program
GAO	General Accounting Office
HAF02	Headquarters Air Force 2002
HQ USAF/XP	Headquarters, United States Air Force Planning and Programming
J-8	The Force Structure, Resources, and Assessment Directorate
IWARS	Integrated Warfighting Architecture Review System
JCS	Joint Chiefs of Staff
JRB	Joint Review Board
JROC	Joint Requirements Oversight Council
JS	Joint Staff
JV	Joint Vision
JVIMP	Joint Vision Implementation Plan
JWCA	Joint Warfighting Capabilities Assessment
LANTFLT	Atlantic Fleet
LRPO	Long-Range Planning Objective
MACOM	Major Command [Army]
MAJCOM	Major Command [Air Force]
MNS	Mission Need Statement

N3/N5	Deputy Chief of Naval Operations (Plans, Policy, and Operations)
N4	Deputy Chief of Naval Operations (Fleet Readiness and Logisics)
N7	Deputy Chief of Naval Operations (Warfare Requirements and Programs)
N8	Deputy Chief of Naval Operations (Resources, Warfare Requirements and Assessments)
N81	Navy Assessment
N75	Expeditionary Warfare Directorate
NDP	National Defense Panel
OPNAV	Office of the Chief of Naval Operations
ORD	Operational Requirements Directives
OSD	Office of the Secretary of Defense
PBD	Program Budget Decision
PD	Program director
PDM	Program Decision Memorandum
PEG	Program Evaluation Groups
PEO	Program Executive Officer
PM	Program Managers
POM	Program Objective Memorandum
PPBES	Planning, Programming, Budgeting, and Execution System
PPBS	Planning, Programming and Budgeting System
QDR	Quadrennial Defense Review
RDTE	Research, Development, Test and Evaluation
SAE	Service acquisition executive
SAF	Secretary of the Air Force

SAF/AQ	Secretary of the Air Force for Acquisition
SECDEF	Secretary of Defense
SECNAV	Secretary of the Navy
TAA	Total Army Analysis
TAP	The Army Plan
USD(A)	Under Secretary of Defense for Acquisition
USD(A&T)	Under Secretary of Defense forAcquisition and Technology
USD(AT&L)	Under Secretary of Defense (Acquisition, Technology & Logistics)
VCJCS	Vice Chairman, Joint Chief of Staff
VCSA	Vice Chief of Staff of the Army
WMD	Weapons of mass destruction
XP	Air Force Plans and Programs Office
XPP	Air Force Directorate of Programs
XPX	Air Force Directorate of Strategic Planning

Chapter One

INTRODUCTION

BACKGROUND

In the fall of 1998, the then–Deputy Director of Air Force Strategic Planning (XPX), Dr. Clark Murdock, requested that Project AIR FORCE assess how the Departments of the Army, Navy, and Air Force perform their planning and programming functions. He wanted to know what types of decision models each of the Services uses for planning and programming and how the models have changed since the passage of the Goldwater-Nichols Department of Defense Reorganization Act of 1986 (P.L. 99-433, popularly known as Goldwater-Nichols). The client also wanted some assessment of the effectiveness of each model in performing planning and programming. The manner in which the various Service headquarters interact with "field" commands, such as the major commands of the Army (MACOMs) and Air Force (MAJCOMs), needed to be examined as well. Dr. Murdock wanted an evaluation of the individual Services' responsiveness to the external demands being placed on them by the Office of the Secretary of Defense (OSD), the Chairman of the Joint Chiefs of Staff (CJCS), the Joint Staff, and Congress. Finally, the client requested an assessment of how the Air Force might improve its planning and programming functions.

This research addresses the issues identified by the project sponsor. The study addresses the evolution of Joint and military decisionmaking since 1986. Among the questions addressed are the following:

1. How have the Goldwater-Nichols legislation and the collapse of the Soviet Union affected decisionmaking within the Department of Defense (DoD)?

2. Why are the acquisition function and its associated decisionmaking disconnected from the Planning, Programming, and Budgeting System (PPBS) process?

3. How have the other Services responded to these changes in their planning and programming functions?

4. How might the Air Force improve its planning, programming, and decisionmaking activities?

ANALYTIC APPROACH

This assessment examines decisionmaking processes within DoD and the Services' interactions with them. It discusses how the "ideal" systems are designed to work. The assessment also provides some insights into how the systems were designed to operate as opposed to how they are actually working.

The most important decisionmaking process, and the one that sets the agenda for DoD, is the PPBS process. The output of the PPBS process determines what DoD should invest in and buy over the next six years. The acquisition function is the next most important decisionmaking process; its purpose is to define "how to buy" the equipment that was identified in the "what to buy" process. The acquisition function is subordinate to the PPBS process. Our research concentrates on the planning and programming functions within the PPBS process; the acquisition function is discussed only insofar as it affects planning and programming decisionmaking processes within a particular Service. For example, it is almost impossible to understand Air Force decisionmaking without some discussion of the dominant role acquisition plays in all phases of resource allocation.

This work builds on prior RAND studies on these topics. The research team interviewed individuals from the Army, Navy, Air Force, Joint Staff, and OSD on the planning, programming, and acquisition processes. The team examined formal and informal documentation relating to how the PPBS and acquisition process have evolved over time. The assessment concentrates on the evolution of the resource environment since the passage of the Goldwater-Nichols legislation, the roles of the Services in the new environment, the increasing complexity of this environment, how the Services have responded, and finally, when necessary, the interactions with the acquisition process. The last section summarizes, provides insights, and makes specific recommendations on how the Air Force might improve its planning and programming processes.

The analytic template used for the assessment is the simple economic model of supply, demand, and integration. Large bureaucracies, such as those found in DoD, need to be structured to be flexible and responsive to internal and external changes and guidance. They must be able to handle complex decisions that consider varying viewpoints. The organization must also accommodate a vertical management structure that is capable of directing and monitoring overall corporate policy. This construct relates to the independence and separability criteria.[1]

The independence criterion states that organizations should be structured so that the choices of resource mixes that one element of the organization makes do not influence those of the other elements. The independence criterion is referred to in operations research as the *decomposition theorem*. This theorem calls for the disaggregation of an entire system into subsystems, each with a small, *independent* subproblem. The theorem asserts that if subsystems interact (i.e., are not independent), solving subproblems will not necessarily yield the correct overall solution.

The multilevel approach posits that one must account for interactions by defining one or more "second-level" subsystems that can aggregate and "objectively" assess the choices identified by the lowest-level subsystem. These choices are aggregated to the next-highest level until the overall solution can be reached at the highest level, thus yielding an overall solution that fully considers the interactions at the lower levels. The construct implies that "good planning practices" require units within organizations to identify their needs and available resources independent of other units.

This construct can be applied both to organizations and information flows within DoD in general and to the military departments specifically. A unit's output (choices) should not influence the input to another unit's planning or choices. If it does, its influence on the

---

[1]The methodology used for this analysis is based on earlier work done by the authors (see Lewis, Roll, et al., 1993).

affected unit or process must be acknowledged and understood by the planners. For example, the independence criterion is violated if the output of one information process is the input of another. The military departments' planning and programming functions can never completely satisfy the independence criterion because often they are directed to perform certain functions as well as told how the directed functions will be performed.

The separability criterion implies that well-informed resource allocations require accomplishing three separate functions independently: an estimation of desired capabilities (within DoD, demand); an estimation of when the resource is available and its cost (supply); and a consideration of the alternatives, their feasibility, and the ultimate costs to an organization if selecting one option over another (integration).

THE PPBS AND ACQUISITION PROCESSES

Much has been written about the PPBS process. The PPBS is DoD's primary system for planning, allocating, and managing defense resources. It links the overall national security strategy to specific programs. The system was designed to facilitate fiscally constrained planning, programming, and budgeting in terms of complete programs (i.e., forces and systems), rather than through artificial budget categories.[2] The goal of the PPBS is to determine force system and program costs by eliciting options and providing for an evaluation of these options in terms of costs and benefits. The output of the process, the defense program, is the official record of major resource allocation decisions made by the Secretary of Defense (SECDEF). This brief discussion describes the "ideal" system and its formal phases and decisionmaking bodies.

The PPBS is one of the SECDEF's essential management tools. The process provides the SECDEF with the means to set and control the department's agenda. The goal is to frame issues in national, rather then Service-specific, terms. The process, which includes documentation and databases, is intended to capture all-important decisions affecting current and future defense budgets.

_____

[2]This discussion is based on previous RAND work (see Lewis, Roll, and Mayer, 1992, and Lewis, Coggin, and Roll, 1994).

There is a funneling aspect to the PPBS (see Figure 1.1). The planning phase starts with broad decisions involving the senior decisionmakers in DoD and progresses to the budgeting phase, where prior decisions are reviewed in detail to determine how they can best be implemented.

Figure 1.2 shows the important PPBS events as they have existed since the implementation of a two-year budget cycle in 1986. In practice, Congress has generally appropriated funds on an annual basis, and therefore the internal DoD process has had to compromise with the demands of producing a budget submission every year. From an external perspective, this behavior could look like the one-year cycle that existed before 1986.

PLANNING PHASE

The new PPBS cycle begins immediately after the budget is submitted to Congress. During the planning phase (the horizon of which may extend 15 years into the future), the existing military posture of the United States is assessed against various concerns, including national security objectives and resource limitations, available military strategies, and the objectives contained in National Security Decision Directives and the National Security Study Directives.

The output of the process is the strategic plan for developing and employing future forces. This plan is defined in the SECDEF's Defense Planning Guidance (DPG), which may be published in the fall or early winter. The DPG contains the SECDEF's top-level guidance for producing the defense program. It is responsive to the President's National Security Strategy, from which the National Military Strategy and fiscal guidance are derived, as set out by the President through the National Security Advisor and the Office of Management and Budget. The DPG may also contain explicit program guidance regarding core programs that the SECDEF wants the Services and DoD agencies to fund in the Program Objective Memoranda (POMs).

Since 1993, CJCS has attempted to influence defense resource guidance and decisionmaking through the development of the chairman's Program Recommendations (CPR). The CPR contains the chairman's recommendations to the SECDEF on programming

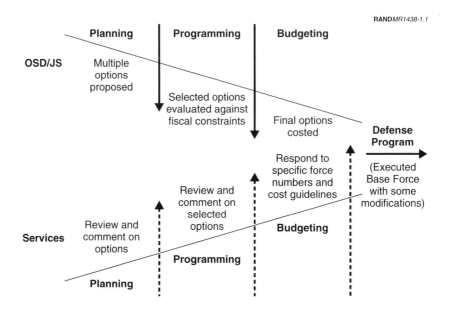

Figure 1.1—The DoD Decisionmaking Process as Shaped by the PPBS

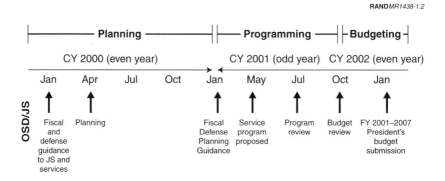

Figure 1.2—The PPBS Time Line of Events

priorities for the DPG. The CPR concentrates on linking forces and equipment in a way that ensures joint operational readiness. The chairman's recommendations are considered by the SECDEF, and some recommendations are then forwarded to the Defense Planning

Advisory Board (DPAG), which is cochaired by the Assistant Secretary of Defense for Strategy and Threats and the Director of Program Analysis and Evaluation (DPA&E). Its members include senior planners and resource managers from OSD, the Services, and the Joint Staff.

PROGRAMMING PHASE

The transition from the planning phase to the programming phase (from the SECDEF's perspective) falls somewhere between the issuance of the DPG in autumn or early winter, and the submittal of the POMs by the military departments and defense agencies in spring. The POMs are Service- and agency-specific resource programs that reflect the DPG and fiscal guidance. The Joint Staff and OSD review the POMs to determine whether the programs meet SECDEF guidance. The programming phase looks five to six years into the future.

The Joint Staff's evaluation of the POMs appears in an internal document, the Chairman's Program Assessment (CPA). The CPA assesses the risks in the forces and equipment proposed by the services and defense agencies in the respective POMs. Included in the assessment is an evaluation of how well the POMs satisfy the requirements identified by the various commanders in chief (CINCs).

OSD reviews the Service POMs and the CPA. If these reviews reveal problems, OSD raises "issues." The problems are then discussed, debated, and resolved within the Defense Resources Board (DRB), which consists of the SECDEF and selected high-level decisionmakers within OSD. Frequently, individuals involved with a particular issue (usually assistant secretaries and Service chiefs) are asked to attend a specific session. Decisions on problem issues are published in the Program Decision Memorandum issued by the Deputy Secretary of Defense (DEPSECDEF).

BUDGETING PHASE

The Program Decision Memorandum marks the end of the programming phase and the beginning of the budgeting phase. The reality is that the military departments and defense agencies have already begun to build detailed budgets by the time they submit their

POMs. After they receive the DEPSECDEF's program decisions, they must adjust their programs and budgets to conform to the decisions. Their programs and budgets are then submitted to the OSD Comptroller in the form of budget estimate submissions, after which budget hearings are held. Major budget issues may be heard in a Defense Program Review Board budget review, with final decisions announced in a series of Program Budget Decisions. The totality of the final versions of these decisions, when used to revise the various budget estimate submissions, becomes the President's budget for DoD, which is submitted to Congress.

THE DoD ACQUISITION PROCESS

The acquisition function is subordinate to the PPBS process; it deals with the "how to buy" question after the PPBS process has decided on "what to buy." DoD acquisition has been a controversial topic since the early 1960s when then-SECDEF Robert McNamara determined that DoD was paying too much for its equipment. Several initiatives were undertaken between the 1960s and 1980s in the hope of making the acquisition function more cost-effective and efficient.[3] The most notable was the report of the President's Blue Ribbon Commission on Defense Management (popularly known as the Packard Commission report), which was followed by congressional passage of the Goldwater-Nichols legislation and the Acquisition Reform Act (ARA). These two pieces of legislation changed the acquisition function.[4]

The Packard Commission report concluded that civilian decision-making authority in DoD needed to be strengthened and that sound military advice needed to be provided to the SECDEF and to the President. The 1986 Goldwater-Nichols legislation adopted and expanded on the report's recommendations. This act moved seven critical functions from military to civilian control and a three-tiered, civilian-controlled acquisition structure was established in the military departments. A civilian acquisition executive managed military Program Executive Officers (PEOs), who managed a portfolio of

---

[3]See Naval War College (1998), Sec. 4.0, for a discussion of various acquisition reform initiatives.

[4]See President's Blue Ribbon Commission on Defense Management (1986).

acquisition programs. Program managers (PMs) reporting to the PEOs on the individual programs in their respective portfolios.

These changes set in motion the development of new and revised deliberative bodies to examine acquisition programs. Most significantly, it empowered the DoD acquisition executive to examine all acquisition programs. Although the legislation was straightforward in that the civilian leadership was now responsible for acquisition decisionmaking, implementing it meant changing many existing decisionmaking bodies and creating new ones.

The objective of the acquisition system is to take the "what to buy" issues, which are an output of the PPBS process, and determine "how they should be bought." The ideal acquisition process ensures that operational capabilities are acquired in a timely manner and at a reasonable cost. It is subordinate to the PPBS process in that it responds to the outputs of the PPBS in terms of purchasing the equipment and capabilities that were identified as required during the PPBS process.

The acquisition process interacts with the PPBS through SECDEF and OSD review of defense programs and through the funding of particular acquisition programs. Figure 1.3 shows the ideal relationship between the PPBS process and the acquisition function within the analytic construct of supply, demand, and integration.

An acquisition program moves through a series of milestones in which the DoD leadership reviews various elements of a particular program, then either gives new guidance or tells the program to continue. There are four acquisition phases, beginning with the approval of a program and its start (Milestone 0) to the fielding of a particular system (Milestone III). The phases associated with each milestone indicate where a particular program is in the DoD pipeline. For example, Milestone 0 and Phase 0 indicate that a need has been identified and that an idea has been put forth that necessitates further study. Phase 0 indicates that the idea is starting to get some definition.[5]

_____

[5]An acquisition program has four milestones (0–III) and four phases. For a detailed discussion of the acquisition process, see Naval War College (1998), pp. 4-3 through 4-7.

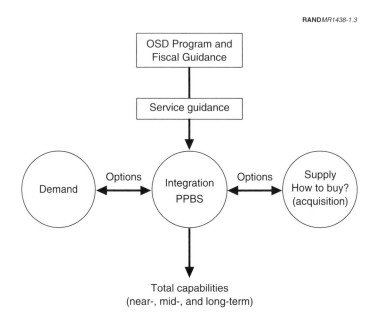

Figure 1.3—Relationship Between PPBS and Acquisition Functions

Defense acquisition programs are divided into three acquisition categories. Acquisition category I (ACAT I) programs are those that are expensive and have high visibility within the defense community. ACAT II and ACAT III programs are major systems but do not have as high a dollar value as ACAT I. For example, ACAT I programs cost around $2.1 billion (FY 1996 constant dollars), while ACAT II programs cost around $640 million (FY 1996 constant dollars).[6] ACAT III programs are those not designated as ACAT I and ACAT II but are those that senior leadership has judged to be important and that thus require careful management.

The SECDEF is the senior decisionmaking authority for the acquisition process within DoD. Three senior advisory boards are involved in shaping the process: The Joint Requirements Oversight Council (JROC) oversees the requirements process; the Defense Acquisition

---

[6]See Naval War College (1998), p. 4-7.

Board (DAB) oversees the Acquisition Management System; and the DRB represents the PPBS oversight of the process.

ORGANIZATION OF THE REPORT

Chapter Two discusses the enactment of the Goldwater-Nichols legislation and ARA. Chapter Three describes how the Goldwater-Nichols legislation affected CJCS and Joint Staff decisionmaking. Chapters Four, Five, and Six describe and assess the decisionmaking processes in each military department, respectively the Army, Navy, and Air Force. Chapter Seven presents the conclusions and recommendations of the report.

Chapter Two

GOLDWATER-NICHOLS AND ACQUISITION REFORM LEGISLATION

Although this report focuses primarily on the military departments' planning and programming functions, it is important to understand the relationship between the PPBS process and the acquisition function. In the Air Force, the acquisition function plays a dominant role in decisionmaking.

THE LEGISLATION

The passage of the Goldwater-Nichols legislation in 1986 fundamentally changed processes and decisionmaking within DoD. The Goldwater-Nichols legislation was passed during a period in which there was a well-understood threat: the Soviet Union. The act thus focused primarily on the development of force structure and weapons to support a major global war with essential objectives in Europe. ARA was a response to the Packard Commission's report, which called for a more cost-effective and efficient acquisition function within DoD. The Goldwater-Nichols legislation directs that the acquisition function be placed under the control of the civilian leadership within the military departments, but ARA further specifies the relationships between the identification of requirements and the development of weapon systems. The military departments responded to each of these laws by reorganizing their staffs and realigning important functions.

The goal of the Goldwater-Nichols legislation was to give the CINCs a stronger voice in defining operational requirements, as well as the resources necessary to perform their missions. The CINCs' spokesperson was the CJCS, whose job it was to integrate CINC requirements, prioritize them, and show how these requirements related to readiness. The CJCS was now responsible for providing independent resource assessments (e.g., readiness to resources) to SECDEF on all matters considered joint, which included requirements, programs, and budget (see Goldwater-Nichols, 1986, and Judge Advocate General, 1999). The CINCs and the CJCS were now directly involved in all phases of planning, programming, and budgeting (Goldwater-Nichols, 1986, re 10 U.S.C. 163 [1][2]).[1] The role of the Services was to provide capabilities to the CINCs to meet their operational requirements. The military departments moved from defining requirements and supplying forces and weapons to providing capabilities to the CINCs. The military departments are responsible for 12 Title 10 functions (Goldwater-Nichols, 1986, Sec. 521), re 10 U.S.C. §8014 [a][c][1]):

1. Recruiting

2. Organizing

3. Supplying

4. Equipping (including research and development)

5. Training

6. Servicing

7. Mobilizing

8. Demobilizing

9. Administering (including the morale and welfare of personnel)

10. Maintaining

11. Construction, outfitting, and repair of military equipment

12. Construction, maintenance, and repair of buildings, structures, and utilities and acquisition of real property.

The Goldwater-Nichols legislation also sought to empower the civilian leadership in OSD and within the military departments. To this end it designated that seven functions, which at the time were under

---

[1]The legislation also directs reexamination and redesign of the PPBS process, specifying that the assessment address whether strategic planning and policy direction is sufficient and consistent with national security strategy, policies, and objectives.

military oversight, be moved to the Service Secretariats: acquisition, auditing, comptroller, information management, inspector general, legislative affairs, and public affairs (Goldwater-Nichols, 1986, Sec. 521, re 10 U.S.C. §8014 [c][1]). Each military department secretary was directed to "designate a single office or entity within his office to conduct each function specified in the legislation"[2] (Goldwater-Nichols, 1986).

The legislation states, for example, that "the Secretary of the Air Force [SAF] has responsibility and authority for carrying out the function of the Department of the Air Force so as to fulfill the current and future operational requirements of the unified and specified combatant commanders." (10 U.S.C. §8013.) The Service staffs were to provide advice, and the Service secretary could determine the relationship of each office or other entity established or designated (Goldwater-Nichols, 1986, re 10 U.S.C. §8014 [2][4]).

The Air Force leadership sought clear definitions of what Chief of Staff of the Air Force (CSAF) and Air Staff "participation" meant in the seven functions moved to the Secretariat and how the CSAF interacted with the SAF in the overall management of the Air Force. On March 24, 1987, the Air Force's General Counsel issued a memorandum attempting to clarify SAF, Chief, and Air Staff responsibilities. It noted that the General Counsel had reviewed the legislation and that the "law does permit elements of the Air Staff to provide advice or assistance to the Chief and otherwise participate in these seven functions under the direction of the office assigned responsibility." (Department of the Air Force, 1987.) The memorandum went on to note that there was little legislative history that could explain "participating" as opposed to conducting a function. The General Counsel then cited the Goldwater-Nichols conference reports, which indicate that these functions could not have offices within the Air Staff but that they could participate in shaping the decisions as long as the Secretariat was responsible for the final decision (Department of the Air Force, 1987).

The legislation blurred a number of other areas, which set up a dynamic between the CJCS and the Service chiefs that continues

---

[2]The ownership of these functions was challenged in the conferences. The relevant conference report reaffirmed the movement of the seven functions to the Service secretariats. See U.S. Congress (September 12, 1986), p. 148.

today. Before the Goldwater-Nichols legislation, for example, Service chiefs predominated in all areas of decisionmaking. They also shaped most decisions within the Joint Chiefs of Staff (JCS), which, although managed by the CJCS, was really another forum in which the Service chiefs asserted their Service prerogatives. The Joint Staff then worked for the JCS. The legislation redirected the Service chiefs' roles. They now provided military advice and perspectives on military requirements to the civilian leadership. Their major mechanism to influence the debate was through the JCS, but now the JCS reported to an empowered CJCS on readiness to resources. The Joint Staff now worked for the CJCS, not for the Service chiefs. Enabling legislation on Joint Staff assignments helped successive chairmen create a powerful and competent staff over time.

One area of contention was about who owns the totality of requirements and who sets the totality of priorities: the CINCs/CJCS or the military departments. The law makes no provision for the intertemporal nature of requirements.

The Army dealt with this issue aggressively. The outgoing Army Chief of Staff (CSA) wrote a letter to the incoming CSA in 1987 outlining the position that the Services own the mid- to long-term requirements inasmuch as they are responsible for providing support to the CINCs in the 12 Title 10 functions designated by the legislation (Wickham, 1987). The CINCs and CJCS were therefore said to be responsible for near-term operational requirements and for identifying the immediate budget requirements.

The Army successfully used this argument with OSD, CJCS, and the other Services. The CINCs and CJCS own operational requirements for the near term, but the Services own the totality of requirements for the near, mid-, and long terms. OSD agreed and provided guidance on this issue. The Services establish priorities for the Title 10 functions for the near, mid-, and long terms; they program and budget for near-, mid- and long-term capabilities. Further agreements were reached within the Goldwater-Nichols conference reports and implementation process.

REORGANIZATION OF THE ACQUISITION FUNCTION

The Goldwater-Nichols legislation and ARA established a civilian-controlled acquisition function within each of the military departments. It is interesting that ARA was drafted and passed without close coordination with the designers of the Goldwater-Nichols legislation. In fact, the drafters of Goldwater-Nichols requested that the ARA legislation be developed in the next Congress in order to give DoD time to implement the Goldwater-Nichols legislation.[3]

The ARA legislation, following what was cited in the Goldwater-Nichols legislation, created a three-tiered, civilian-controlled acquisition function (Goldwater-Nichols, 1986). All DoD acquisition was to be overseen by a civilian acquisition executive, the Under Secretary of Defense for Acquisition (USD[A]).[4] The USD(A) position, however, was not clearly defined. To be sure, it had broad purview— it was responsible for all acquisition matters and was intended to streamline the acquisition organization and procedures by facilitating communication between PMs and acquisition officials—but exactly how all these functions fit together was not well articulated in the legislation (Roll, 1989).

The three-tiered acquisition structure was also imposed in the military departments and defense agencies on all programs Goldwater-Nichols and ARA defined as major—that is, any DoD programs that exceeded $10 million or were determined to be selected acquisition programs. These programs were referred to as ACAT I and II, and selected major programs. A senior procurement executive, who was also to function as the Service acquisition executive (SAE), was given the responsibility for the management and direction of each Service's acquisition system. This included the implementation of the unique procurement policies, regulations, and standards of the executive agency (41 U.S.C. §414 [3]). Selected acquisition programs reported to PEOs, who reported to the SAE. In turn, PMs and program directors reported to the PEOs.

Each military department realigned its functions in response to its definitions of the legislation and its impacts. In late 1988, Congress requested that the General Accounting Office (GAO) review the status of the military Services' acquisition reorganization initiatives in order

---

[3]Interview with Archie D. Barrett, former congressional staff member, September 1998.

[4]The position has since been redesignated as the Under Secretary of Defense for Acquisition, Technology, and Logistics (USD[AT&L]).

to assess whether the departments' restructuring complied with the intent of the Goldwater-Nichols legislation (GAO, 1989).

In June 1989, a GAO report noted that the Army was the most compliant with the legislation and its intents. The report further noted that the Navy had been only partially responsive to the legislation. Although the Air Force had reorganized its headquarters acquisition management structure, the report found that the acquisition function continued to be predominantly staffed with military officers and did not comply with the intent of the legislation (GAO, 1989). The Air Force argued that the Secretariat was in charge of acquisition, as was the strategic decisionmaking associated with the function. It was argued that the military officers were advising and participating in the function in accordance with the 1987 Air Force General Counsel memorandum and the conference reports' interpretation of the law. The SECDEF disagreed.

Concurrent with the GAO review (in February 1989), President George H. W. Bush asked then-SECDEF Richard Cheney to provide him with an assessment of how DoD might improve its defense procurement process. The SECDEF's Directed Management Review (DMR) report, released on July 11, 1989,[5] contained ten recommendations, four of which discussed the procurement process:

1. The USD(A) exercises full authority for major acquisition programs through streamlined Service organizations consisting of SAEs, PEOs, and PMs.

2. With a simplified and more efficient acquisition structure, DoD must eliminate layers and functions that add no value, with the goal of a $7.5 billion reduction in annual cost by FY 1993.

3. The USD(A) must manage a more disciplined process for reviewing major weapon programs as they proceed through the stages of development, testing, and fielding.

4. DoD must take steps to improve its management of civilian and military acquisition personnel, including establishing in each military department a dedicated corps of military officers who will be career acquisition specialists.

---

[5]As recorded in working papers for the DoD DMR, July 11, 1989.

The recommendations for improvement were contained in a DMR issued on July 11, 1989. In addition to the four acquisition changes, the DMR also made recommendations on changing the OSD DAB. It directed the DAB to review requirements, cost trade-offs, initial affordability assessments, and other minimum required accomplishments at the concept approval phase (Milestone I). It further directed that concept approval not be given to any new programs until long-term funding has been determined and assured in the budget.

The acquisition reform initiative was implemented through the rewriting of the DoD directive on acquisition; it is called DoD Directive 5000.1, "Defense Acquisition." The 5000 series, which was rewritten in 1989, 1994, 1996, 1999, and 2000, establishes the guidelines for the acquisition function. The 1989 directive and all those following identified the Under Secretary of Defense for Acquisition and Technology (USD[A&T]) as the senior acquisition executive of DoD. He is the senior and principal advisor to the SECDEF and DEPSECDEF for all matters relating to the DoD acquisition system, research and development, advanced technology, test and evaluation, production, logistics, military construction, procurement, economic security, environmental security, and atomic energy (DoD, Directive 5134.1, 2000). The USD(A&T) executes his responsibility through interactions with all levels of DoD. He interacts with the CJCS to ensure that joint requirements are being addressed in the acquisition programs that he supports. The CJCS was designated, and the 5000 series supported the use of the JROC as the authority to review and validate operational shortfalls and Service responses. The JROC is the validation and approval authority for the Mission Need Statements (MNSs) as they work their way through the Requirements Generation System (within the Services and OSD). The JROC charter indicates that it reviews only the MNSs that may become ACAT I, ACAT II, or selected special programs. Upon approval, the JROC forwards the MNSs to the DAB for consideration. After the DAB decides that a program will be initiated, the JROC continues to evaluate that program as it proceeds through the acquisition process.

Chapter Three

IMPLEMENTATION AND EVOLUTION OF THE CURRENT DECISIONMAKING PROCESSES, 1986–1999

Before the implementation of the Goldwater-Nichols legislation, the Services were responsible both for identifying CINC operational requirements and for providing the capabilities. Congress believed that the influence of the Services and, in particular, of the military leadership had become too powerful and that a more balanced perspective was needed. The Goldwater-Nichols legislation attempted to further implement the model of centralized decisionmaking and decentralized execution.[1] The goal of the legislation was to strengthen the role of the operational commanders in resource decisionmaking through the empowerment of the CJCS. The CJCS was to represent the CINCs in articulating operational requirements and in ensuring the necessary funding. The legislation also sought to strengthen civilian control of DoD. Since 1986, the decisionmaking processes within DoD have become increasingly complex. In part, this complexity is attributable to a number of new activities that have been established in support of the development of joint operational capabilities and their resourcing.

---

[1]The decision model is important because Congress attempted to institutionalize it. Earlier SECDEFs had tried different models, much to the consternation of the Services and Congress. For example, in the 1960s, Secretary Robert McNamara attempted to institutionalize decisionmaking and execution. During the Nixon administration, Secretary Melvin Laird attempted to implement a highly decentralized model. In the early 1980s, Secretary Caspar Weinberger's Deputy, Frank Carlucci, sought to implement centralized decisionmaking and decentralized execution. This is the model the Packard Commission and ultimately, Congress, recommended. These events are described in the Laird working papers, the Carlucci initiatives and working papers, and the Packard Commission report (1986).

This chapter discusses some of the changes that have occurred in the Joint Staff and OSD. Subsequent chapters will address Service responses, with particular emphasis on the Air Force.

CJCS AND JOINT STAFF EVOLUTION

The Goldwater-Nichols legislation specified that the CJCS is to provide independent assessments to the SECDEF on readiness, operational requirements, and resourcing. On the basis of this charter, the Joint Staff's activities have gradually expanded to include active participation in the planning, programming, and budgeting process. The evolutionary route of the Joint Staff's involvement in the PPBS has resulted in the definition of new processes and the refocusing of some existing processes and forums. The Gulf War accelerated the direct involvement of the Joint Staff in resourcing because it confirmed to many in Congress and OSD that military and civilian decisionmaking was balanced and working. The CJCS's role in ensuring that readiness is properly resourced is essential to the development of a post–Cold War military and has been an important justification for further involvement of the CJCS and his staff in the PPBS process.[2]

The evolution of the CPA and CPR processes also illustrates the expansion of the Joint Staff's involvement in all aspects of the PPBS and acquisition processes. In response to being responsible for providing an independent assessment of the SECDEF on how operational capabilities are being resourced, the CJCS revitalized the CPA in 1989.[3] The CPA now reviews each of the Service programs at the end of the programming phase and provides feedback to the SECDEF on whether CINC requirements have been appropriately funded to meet near-, mid-, and long-term readiness goals. The CPA has thus become an important source of information for the SECDEF as he queries the Services during the program review phase (CJCS, 1997).

---

[2]10 U.S.C. 153(a)(3)(c) directs the CJCS to advise the SECDEF on critical deficiencies and strengths in force capabilities identified during the preparation and review of CINC contingency plans. See GAO (1990).

[3]Although the CJCS had always provided an assessment of programs, the Goldwater-Nichols legislation mandated that this be done. It was not until 1989 that the CJCS decided to make the CPA a robust and important document in assessing the Services' programs. See Schwabe, Lewis, and Schrader (1996).

For the sake of effectiveness, the Vice Chairman of the Joint Chiefs of Staff (VCJCS) and the CJCS decided that they needed to influence the Service resource allocation processes proactively. The J-8 thus initiated the CPR assessment to provide an independent evaluation of the critical joint operational capabilities that are needed to support CINC missions.[4] Its objective is to influence the DPG, which in turn informs the Services of DoD's resourcing priorities and directs how the Services are to address the priorities in their respective POMs. To enhance joint readiness, provide new operational capabilities, and promote joint doctrine and training, CPR makes recommendations on which systems should be funded and on their relative priority. It also recommends which Service programs should be downsized or canceled from a joint perspective.[5] The CPR and CPA are now part of OSD's formal planning and programming processes (Naval War College, 1998, pp. 2-1 through 2-3).[6]

The CJCS and his staff concluded in 1994 that a joint vision was essential to the development of joint capabilities. Shortly thereafter, Joint Vision 2010 (JV 2010) was published. JV 2010 has also had a profound influence on the Services' ability to identify mid- to long-term requirements. Indeed, the document is now considered a capstone piece in which Service visions and programs must demonstrate that they are meeting the objectives of JV 2010/2020 on how future warfighting will be conducted. First published in 1995, JV 2010 defines future operational concepts and offers guidance on what core capabilities the Services need to provide to support joint warfighting in the near, mid-, and long terms. The document identifies four joint operational capabilities: dominant maneuver, precision engagement, focused logistics, and full-dimension protection. JV 2010 has moved the CJCS from advising the SECDEF on current joint operational requirements and their relative priority to one in

---

[4]This was described in J-8's working papers on the development of the CPR and in an interview with LTC Francis Finelli (USA Ret.), May 1999; see also CJCS (1997b).

[5]The CPR is quite specific about what capabilities need to be acquired and in what quantities. It also tends to address what is required or what is insufficient rather than what the Services should divest themselves of. See CJCS (1997a, 1998, and 1999).

[6]The Joint Planning Document, which is based on the CPR and CPA, provides the early planning and broad programming advice to the SECDEF. This document is also used to inform the JROC and Joint Warfighting Capabilities Assessment (JWCA) teams about CJCS programming priorities. See CJCS (1997b).

which the Joint Staff identifies the mid- and long-term strategic operational concepts for DoD and outlines how the Services must respond to them. This process was further matured with the 1997 publication of the Joint Vision Implementation Plan (JVIMP), which provides a road map for how the capabilities identified in JV2010 will be attained (CJCS, 1999a).[7]

The Joint Staff has encouraged the Services to continue their own institutional vision work and strategic planning activities, but these activities must be responsive to JV 2010 and the JVIMP. Although there is no formal legislation or DoD regulation that requires the Services to support or respond to JV 2010 and the JVIMP, several supporting processes have evolved and old ones have been redefined that have reinforced the goals and objectives laid out in the two documents. In 1999, JV 2010 was updated and redesignated JV 2020. Currently, all the Service visions and strategic plans make explicit linkages to JV 2020, the JVIMP, and now joint experimentation. The CJCS issued a formal instruction in 1999 that described his role in the PPBS process (CJCS, 1999a). The revised instruction identifies JV 2010 and its implementation initiative.

The establishment of the JWCA process in 1994 and the refocusing of the Joint Requirements Oversight Council in 1995 furthered the Joint Staff's direct involvement in the PPBS process and, more significantly, increased its involvement in the "what to buy" debate.

The JWCA process began in 1995 as a partial response to the frustration of the then-VCJCS over what he viewed as the lack of responsiveness of the Services and defense agencies in meeting joint operational demands. Initially, the JWCA process identified eight broad mission categories and functions that were deemed critical to joint operational capabilities and readiness.[8] The process was designed to provide the CJCS with information on readiness and an ability to independently identify and assess CINC requirements toward the

---

[7]JVIMP 2001 is an updated version of the earlier document.

[8]The initial JWCA ribbons or panels as of August 1995 were Strike; Land and Littoral Warfare; Strategic Mobility of Sustainability; Sea, Air, and Space Superiority; Deter/Counter Proliferation of Weapons of Mass Destruction; Command and Control; Joint Readiness; Intelligence, Surveillance, and Reconnaissance; Regional Engagement/Presence; Information Warfare; Joint Vision 2010; and the JROC/JWCA Process.

goal of informing the CPR and JROC processes.[9] Today, it is another element of the PPBS process and is formally identified in process and organizational charts as providing a direct input into the JROC capability shortfalls and future operational requirements.

By 1998, there were 13 JWCA assessment areas or ribbons.[10] Some of the new categories reflect the gradual expansion of the Joint Staff into what were traditionally viewed as Service prerogatives. In 1997, for example, the Infrastructure and Reform Initiatives ribbons were established. The Infrastructure JWCA is chartered to examine Service infrastructure and to assess its ability to support readiness. This ribbon is a direct outgrowth of the 1996–1997 Quadrennial Defense Review (QDR), in which the military departments, seeking to prevent proposed OSD infrastructure reductions, directly linked infrastructure to operational readiness. This linkage gave the Joint Staff entry into examining infrastructure as part of joint operational capabilities and readiness.[11] The Reform Initiative ribbon assesses the potential impacts of the Defense Reform Initiative and Defense Management Council activities, as well as those of any other reform initiatives on warfighting capabilities and readiness. The Joint Readiness ribbon attempts to provide an integrative look at the ability of Service personnel management and force management systems, exercises, training, and related activities and systems to deliver adequate and timely support to the CINCs.

In summer 2000, the Joint Staff initiated a review of the JWCA ribbons and concluded that the both ribbons and their phases had become too large and cumbersome. The Joint Staff then collapsed several of the ribbons and defined new ones, resulting in the following current list:

1. Dominant Maneuver

2. Precision Engagement

---

[9]See memorandum for the JROC Review Board (1996)

[10]As of October 1999, the current JWCA ribbons had expanded to include Reform Initiatives, Joint Readiness, and Infrastructure. See CJCS (1999b).

[11]The QDR occurred from 1996 to May 1997. The review attempted to have DoD answer a series of questions that Congress had posed in its frustration with the slowness of the Services' transformation from a Cold War to a post–Cold War military. The National Defense Panel (NDP) reviewed the QDR's outputs and concluded that the transformation of DoD was far too slow. See NDP (1997).

3. Information Superiority

4. Focused Logistics

5. Full Dimensional Protection

6. Command, Control and Communications and Computer Environment

7. Intelligence Surveillance, and Reconnaissance

8. Strategic Deterrence.

The JROC has oversight over the JWCA process with the assistance of the Joint Review Board (JRB). The JROC charter gives it the responsibility to examine all aspects of defense resource allocation as part of CJCS's responsibility to provide independent assessments to the SECDEF on operational capabilities and readiness (see CJCS, 2001). The JROC is directed to identify and assess the priority of joint military requirements (including existing systems and equipment) and has direct input into the DoD acquisition process through the DAB. It is chaired by the VCJCS and consists of the vice chiefs from each of the military departments and invited guests. The JROC has gradually become involved not only in examining proposed alternatives to operational concepts and required capabilities but also in assessing "how to buy" proposals from the Services. On a regular basis, it now validates requirements and examines the cost, schedule, and performance criteria of a program, as well as aspects of the procurement plan. More recently, its activities have expanded into assessing and making recommendations on how the Services man and train for new missions and for new capabilities coming into the inventory. The body has directed a stronger examination of the Command, Control, Communications, Computers, Intelligence, Surveillance, and Reconnaissance Master Plan, as well as specific Service-proposed capabilities.[12]

---

[12]Generally, the meetings are closed, with the outcomes shared only within the specific Services. Some recent JROC issues have been a directed reexamination of the Army's Crusader system, a heavy field artillery system; an examination of lift requirements that has resulted in the Mobility Requirements Study 2005, and an examination of joint interdiction systems. The new JROC charter shows the breadth and scope of the JROC into policy, PPBS, and requirements decisionmakers. This work is being done under an expanded view of what constitutes "requirements." See Joint Requirements Instruction.

The expansion of the JROC's activities into both the "what to buy" and "how to buy" arenas has in part resulted from its expanded role during the QDR. During that process, the JROC was used as a forum to vet major DoD issues before such issues went to the CJCS, JCS, and SECDEF. Legislation in the Defense Authorization Act of 1996 further expanded the role of the JROC to setting operational requirements and determining future acquisition funding (Defense Authorization Act of 1996). The JROC charter and instruction have been revised to reflect these important shifts in responsibility.

It is significant to note that the JROC, although initially not an official part of any decisionmaking system within the PPBS process, is now closely tied to and supports nearly all the major decisionmaking bodies associated with that process. In part, the JROC's expanded role is buttressed by the all-encompassing JWCA process and the JRB. As part of its regular work, the JROC tracks acquisition programs to assess their ability over time to be responsive to the joint operational environment. The JRB was established by the JROC to oversee and integrate the JWCA process. Its job is to further refine, shape, and develop issues, based on the JWCA's findings, into topics appropriate for the JROC. It is not unusual for the JRB, through its review and shaping of the JWCA work, to ask for Service assessments of a particular acquisition program and the sustainment issues associated with readiness. It now functions as a clearinghouse for all JROC agenda items.[13]

The playing field became more complex with the growing involvement of the CINCs in both planning and programming. In 1995, General George Joulwan, CINC, European Command, argued in a letter to the CJCS and the SECDEF that DoD planning and programming must address "the other missions" that the CINCs are being asked to perform. General Joulwan maintained that resources were not connected to the reality of missions and that the Joint Staff must take the initiative to ensure that DoD is responsive to "resourcing the totality of CINC missions" (Joulwan, 1995).

This issue continues to emerge in both the JWCA processes and in meetings of the JROC. In the 1996–1997 QDR, the growing complex-

---

[13]Service interviews, Air Force, August 1999; Army, October 1, 1999.

ity of the operational environment and the Services' ability to respond to these demands were further challenged. The J-8 Dynamic Commitment (DC) games revealed that the CINCs disagreed with Service-provided capabilities to support a wide range of operations.[14] In part, the deputy CINCs' response grew out of the work done by the CINCs' planning staffs, which identified what joint capabilities the theater needed to support various operations. Many CINCs are forming strategic planning cells that identify near-, mid-, and long-term operational requirements. These organizations work closely with the CINCs' operational planning staffs, who are now doing concepts of operation for all missions that might emerge within the CINCs' areas of responsibility per the Joint Strategic Capabilities Process and SECDEF guidance. The outputs of these activities inform the Joint Staff processes and directly involve the CINCs in DoD planning and programming.

INTEGRATION OF OSD, JOINT STAFF, AND CINC ACTIVITIES

The evolutionary expansion of the Joint Staff into active participation in the "what to buy" and "how to buy" questions has been buttressed by the linkage of PPBS and acquisition decisionmaking at the OSD levels through the DRB and modifications to the DoD 5000 series regulations. DoD Directive 5000.1, the governing document on defense acquisition, notes that the acquisition function translates "broadly stated mission needs into well-defined system-specific requirements and ultimately into operationally effective, suitable and survivable systems" (DoD, 1996, p. 2). Sustainment issues have now been linked through 5000.1, stating that the acquisition system is to "acquire quality products that satisfy the needs of the operational user with measurable improvements to mission accomplishment" (DoD, 1996, Sec. D [Policy], pp. 3–4). The gradual blurring of the "what to buy" and "how to buy" questions has occurred as the

---

[14]The DC games were a series of four quality tabletop games that J-8 ran within the Joint Staff to attempt to determine what operational requirements were being imposed on the Services and what sufficiency each Service had to meet these demands. In DC3 (January 1997), the deputy CINCs argued that the Services were sending the wrong capabilities, as well as too many forces and equipment, to the theater. This criticism was leveled particularly at the Army. See Schrader, Lewis, and Brown (1999).

Joint Staff and CINCs push to address "tooth to tail" issues within the context of operational capabilities, readiness, and costs in all forums in which they participate. In particular, the CJCS's and VCJCS's involvement in both the DRB and the DAB has begun to challenge the Service chiefs' and secretaries' traditional roles in making the "what to buy" decisions.

For example, the DRB makes major planning and programming decisions and is chaired by the SECDEF. The board's activities have also expanded into providing direction on the DPG, as well as reviewing Service POMs. The CJCS is a sitting member of the DRB and provides an important crosswalk between the Joint Staff processes—JWCA/JROC and readiness assessments—and OSD. The DRB, along with the Joint Staff processes, now formally links the "what to buy" with the "how to buy" and then links both to joint operational requirements and readiness.

DAB has also contributed to the blurring of the "what to buy" and "how to buy" issues. The DAB's vice chairman is the VCJCS. The VCJCS is the only person who sits on every panel at the OSD and Joint Staff levels who looks across the totality of DoD activities: requirements, prioritization of requirements, the assessment of "what to buy" and "how to buy." It is not a surprise that the separation of the "what to buy" and "how to buy" questions have become more blurred over time within DoD.

The evolutionary process of implementing the Goldwater-Nichols legislation has also begun to blur the tacit agreement reached in the late 1980s among the OSD, CJCS, and Services—in effect, that the CINCs and CJCS own warfighting requirements for the near term, while the Services own the totality of Title 10 requirements for the near, mid-, and long terms. The NDP, which assessed the outcomes of the 1997 QDR, stated in its report that the Services are too steeped in individual prerogatives to transition into post–Cold War forces (NDP, 1997). The NDP report recommended and OSD, in late 1997, supported the concept of joint experimentation as the mechanism by which to address the prevailing Service-centric approaches. The Defense Authorization Act for 1998 assigned responsibility for the development of the Joint Warfighting Experiments to the Atlantic Command. Recent legislation has now renamed the Atlantic Command as the U.S. Joint Forces Command.[15] What is not clear with the emergence of this joint command is whether the military departments will continue to generate the operational concepts or respond to the concept assessment and development of the Joint Staff and Joint Forces commander. However, the advanced concept technology demonstration (ACTD) programs that are being centrally managed within OSD may provide a hint.

Approximately 46 ACTD programs that span weapons, communications, and sensors were defined in 1998 (Eash, 1998). The goal of the ACTDs is to decide both "what to buy" and "how to buy it" through what is termed the streamlining of the acquisition function. The ACTDs are to develop a concept and demonstrate the technology that would enable a capability to be developed. The ACTDs emphasize the integration of existing technology into an operational concept. They also have the ability to initiate production within the acquisition process, although they are not a substitute for that process (see Eash, 1998, p. 36). The ACTD activity is shaped around the joint operational capabilities identified in JV 2010 and JV 2020. Since their initiation, many have failed or been terminated. Others continue and have led to a variety of new acquisition initiatives.

This assessment of CJCS and Joint Staff activities does not suggest that the CJCS, the Joint Staff, and OSD have been systematic in their development of new or modified decisionmaking forums or that the increased involvement of the CJCS and the Joint Staff in resource decisionmaking is wrong. Rather, the evolution has been gradual and has occurred in an environment in which many processes operate independent of one another. This causes subtle shifts in the playing field to go almost unnoticed in a period of staff downsizing, decreases in defense budgets, and increased deployments. For example, the acquisition function operates almost entirely outside the PPBS process in terms of its key decision points, milestones, and funding streams. Often, acquisition personnel view themselves as a separate process from the PPBS. To them, the PPBS is responsible only for providing sufficient funding to develop selected systems. A lack of discipline within DoD has further contributed to this misconception.

---

[15]"Joint Forces Command Assumes Future Area of Responsibility" (1999).

What we are observing, however, is DoD's gradual movement away from the Goldwater-Nichols model of centralized and decentralized decisionmaking and decentralized execution to one of centralized and decentralized decisionmaking and centralized execution. In part, this evolution has occurred because the Services are viewed by OSD, the CJCS/Joint Staff, and some members of Congress as being too slow in their transformation from a Cold War to a post–Cold War military. Some critics point to important Service procurement programs, such as the Air Force's F-22 fighter, the Army's Comanche helicopter, and the Navy's Aegis destroyer. Individual Services started all these programs in the 1980s and continue to support them despite changes in the geostrategic environment, in which there is no peer competitor now or in the foreseeable future and in which huge costs are associated with each program. These systems, however, are still years away from full operational fielding.

Confusion over the type of decisionmaking that dominates DoD is also attributable to the development of consensus-built decisionmaking within DoD. Consensus-built decisionmaking involves all participants and usually safeguards the equities of each. Management literature points out that consensus-built decisionmaking reduces most decisions to the margins because, in the interest of getting agreement, most of the hardest issues are either not addressed or pushed aside, having been deemed too hard to adjudicate (Waterman, 1992; Lewis, 1966). The most recent example of this consensus-built decisionmaking is the 1997 QDR. The QDR never addressed the tough questions facing DoD; rather, it avoided such key issues as force structure and force size, as well as investment and divestiture, either by not discussing them at all or by concluding that the status quo was sufficient (Lewis and Roll, 2000).

This assessment has discussed the rise of the CJCS and Joint Staff in terms of participation in all levels of DoD decisionmaking. This increased involvement has not always resulted in better decisionmaking or in clarity of purpose. The changes have resulted in the Services modifying and changing their decisionmaking processes to accommodate the Joint perspective and clout.

Chapter Four

ARMY DECISIONMAKING PROCESSES

The Army was the most responsive of the three Services to the changes directed by the Goldwater-Nichols legislation.[1] The Army leadership established a study group, composed primarily of members of the Army Staff (ARSTAF), to determine how the legislation was to be implemented. Financial management and acquisition were the two functions most affected by the passage of Goldwater-Nichols legislation and its subsequent implementation by the Army.

Initially, the Army viewed the relocation of financial management to the Secretariat as simply requiring that the existing office in ARSTAF report to the Assistant Secretary of Army for Financial Management and Comptroller (ASA[FM&C]). One difficulty was that the Army Budget Office (ABO) fell under the comptroller function; the ABO position was managed by a lieutenant general, whose duties overlapped those of the newly appointed civilian assistant secretary. The ABO position was eventually downgraded to that of a two-star who reported to the assistant secretary.

More problematic, however, was how the responsibilities associated with the programming and budgeting phases of the PPBS were to be managed. The designers of the reorganization did not take into account the overlapping aspects of programming and budgeting activities and therefore did not assess the existing processes so that potential impacts could be determined prior to the reorganization. Instead, they viewed the programming phase as distinctly separate

---

[1]GAO (1989) indicated that the Army had responded to the legislation, while the Air Force and the Navy had not fully complied by that time.

from the budgeting phase.[2] The redesign therefore concluded that the Army Comptroller should manage all budgeting issues, while programming remained the purview of DPA&E. The Army leadership only discovered these problems while it was building its 1989–1996 POM, published in 1988. During this periodt, it found that its deliberative bodies, databases, and decisionmaking could not be as distinct and separate as had initially been thought. The resulting POM-development process followed pre–Goldwater-Nichols legislation patterns in that the ARSTAF developed the program and directed how it should be budgeted.

The newly appointed civilian leadership for the Army further affected the implementation of the legislation in 1992. The civilian leadership concluded from the outset that the Goldwater-Nichols legislation should be fully implemented. Basing its view on a strict legal interpretation of the legislation, the civilian leadership held that the CSA and the ARSTAF were subordinate to the Secretary of the Army and that the Secretary of the Army was ultimately responsible for all decisionmaking. In this view, the Army Comptroller was in charge of the PPBS process and was directly responsible for all decisions associated with the development and presentation of the budget.[3] One result of this conclusion was an ongoing tension from 1992 to 1999 between the Secretary of the Army and the ARSTAF over roles and responsibilities. Another result is that members of the Secretariat became increasingly vocal about being excluded from key decision forums. The members argued that, since Army decisionmaking was hierarchical, excluding them at the lower levels of the decision hierarchy limited Secretariat input, thereby denying the secretary full visibility into and knowledge of a particular issue.

---

[2]The planning phase was never addressed in the realignment, since it was not mentioned in the legislation. It remained in the Office of the Deputy Chief of Staff for Operations and Plans (DCSOPS).

[3]In early 1993, the Army Secretariat appointed a commission to study the roles and responsibilities of the Secretariat vis-à-vis the military staff. The study concluded that the critical functions, processes, and decisionmaking should reside in the Secretariat (see Blumenfeld, 1994). To curtail some of the debate, the Army Secretariat and ARSTAF agreed to amend the Army regulation, putting ASA(FM&C) in charge of the overall PPBS process. The regulation gave ASA(FM&C) oversight of only the PPBS process, not the specific functions. In particular, the planning and programming functions remained in the ARSTAF. See Army Regulations 11-32 (Army, 1989a) and 10-1 (Army, 1989b), and see Judge Advocate General (1993).

In response to these criticisms, the ARSTAF has redesigned many of its processes and decisionmaking bodies to include members of the Secretariat. Currently, most decisionmaking bodies for planning, programming, and budgeting include the appropriate members from the Secretariat and the ARSTAF necessary for hierarchical decision-making. The oversight of the Planning, Programming, Budgeting, and Execution System (PPBES) process was placed under the ASA (FM&C).[4]

The Army's acquisition function has undergone substantial change in response to the Goldwater-Nichols legislation. The initial imple-mentation resulted in the placement of the acquisition function, procurement, and Research, Development, Test, and Evaluation monies in the office of the newly formed Army Senior Acquisition Executive. The Army rigorously adhered to a strict interpretation of the Goldwater-Nichols legislation in that a separate three-tiered acquisition function with clear lines of responsibility to the Service acquisition executive was established. The Service, however, contin-ued to rely on the Army Materiel Command to provide acquisition support in the form of labor and infrastructure. The logistics func-tion is also handled within this command. The Deputy Chief of Staff for Logistics provides headquarters oversight on logistics policy and program issues. In 1998, the Assistant Secretary of the Army for Installations, Logistics, and Environment turned over all logistics responsibilities to the Deputy Chief of Staff for Logistics; the Defense Logistics Agency; and the Army Materiel Command, renaming his position to Assistant Secretary of the Army for Installations and Envi-ronment (ASA[I&E]).

ARMY PLANNING AND PROGRAMMING

The Army's resource decision model reflects its resourcing focus on force structure (FS) and end strength (ES).[5] The Army's model is cen-tralized decisionmaking and decentralized execution. The Army

---

[4]See the discussion in draft Army Regulation 10-1 (1989b).

[5]*Force structure* refers to the number of divisions and their associated components: brigades and battalions. *End strength* refers to the actual number of people in the Army—Active and Reserve—at any one time. The Army bases its end strength on the need to fill units and support the institutional Army. See U.S. Army War College (1998), pp. 5-31 through 5-33.

headquarters provides planning and programming guidance to the field and operating agencies; the MACOMs and field agencies respond primarily with budget inputs. The Total Army Analysis (TAA)[6] process determines the size and makeup of the future force. The goal of the process is to identify the total nonfiscally constrained requirement for FS and ES. After the objective force is determined, some fiscal constraints are applied to ensure that the Army's FS and ES demands are at least responsive to the fiscal guidance from OSD.

Until 2000, the DCSOPS dominated all resource decisionmaking within the Army because he owned the FS/ES and modernization portfolios. He was in charge of setting the total priorities for all Army resources as well as ensuring that near-term operational demands were met. In 2000, the modernization portfolio was given to the Assistant Vice Chief of Staff, Army (AVCSA), and that position was then given the new title of Deputy Chief of Staff for Programs (DCSPRO). The DCSPRO is now responsible for the development of the Army program, but the DCSOPS retains FS/ES and the prioritization of requirements for the total Army.

The ARSTAF is organized along the warfighting functions associated with the division structure: operations and plans, intelligence, personnel, modernization, logistics, reserve affairs, etc. The ARSTAF's organization was established during World War II; although it underwent some modifications as a result of directed staff reductions and some minor staff reorganizations, it survived intact until the 1999 reorganization (Hewes, 1975). All ARSTAF issues are addressed within the individual functional stovepipes. For example, JWCA and JROC activities have been accommodated within

---

[6]The TAA process defines the total force, which includes the "below the line," echelon above division/echelon above corps, combat, combat support, and combat service support. In 1997, the TAA process was redesigned after OSD arguments that the assessment was used to justify a large Army force structure and end strength. The revised TAA process uses a new Army-developed methodology, the Mission Organization Task Force System, that provides a total accounting of all Army forces: Tables of Organization and Equipment, which include all the warfighting elements of the Army, and Tables of Distribution and Allowances. The TAA process defines the total requirement for Army forces; its initial outputs are nonfiscally constrained. Eventually the Army applies some fiscal constraints to the total FS/ES requirements and informs OSD of its total needs and the costs associated with the requirements. See U.S. Army War College (1998); this is also discussed in the Army's working papers on the system's methodology dated June 1999.

the existing functional structure. Joint actions are handled through the DCSOPS' Force Development—Joint Actions (DAMO-FD) organization and are shared with the DCSPRO. The DAMO-FD office is responsible for keeping the Vice Chief of Staff, Army (VCSA) informed as to the outputs of the JWCAs and JRB meetings and for preparing the VCSA for JROC sessions.

Like the other Services, the Army headquarters has undergone several OSD-directed staff reductions. The 40-percent staff reduction between fiscal years 1992 and 1999 was particularly hard on the Army because reductions were allocated symmetrically across the ARSTAF and the Secretariat, not because the Army leadership had rethought the processes and headquarters organization (GAO, 1999). The leadership acknowledges that the additional directed 25-percent reduction to be taken between FY 2000 and FY 2002 will "break the staff's back" unless some reorganization is done. In 1991, in response to directed staff reductions, the Assistant Deputy Chief of Staff for Operations (ADCSOPS) directed that Army long-range planning be discontinued. The Army would rely on the Joint Strategy Review to provide its planning guidance.[7] The ADCSOPS concluded that Army planning had little value given that the TAA process that responded to Army-generated requirements determined FS and ES.[8]

ARMY REENGINEERING INITIATIVES

In 1995, the Secretary of the Army and the CSA concluded that the Army planning and programming functions were not providing sufficient information for decisionmaking. Both OSD and the Joint Staff had criticized the Army's 1997–2002 program as not being responsive to joint operational demands.[9] OSD and the Joint Staff also argued that the Army should show how it built its program and what tradeoffs had been made to ensure that the program was balanced and met the external guidance. The Secretary of the Army further concluded that it wanted increased participation in resource decisionmaking. Since the Army is a hierarchical decisionmaking institution,

---

[7]This is discussed in the Army's long-range planning working papers of 1998 and 1999.

[8]Interview with LTC Robert Snyder, DAMO Strategy-Planning, September 1998.

[9]For a history of why the Army wanted to reengineer its processes, see Lewis, Brown, and Schrader (1999).

the Secretariat sought to ensure that it participated at each critical decision level rather than only at the highest levels of the institution.

In 1995, the Army's model for decisionmaking focused on satisfying the large demand established by the DCSOPS, who established the resourcing priorities for the Army. The DCSOPS focused primarily on providing capabilities—forces and systems—for current operations. Army Program Analysis and Evaluation (PA&E) had the responsibility for resourcing the priorities determined by the DCSOPS. The requirements that were not funded were identified as the critical program shortfalls, but only because they were unfunded requirements; they were not assessed in terms of their relative importance to the Army's overall ability to provide capabilities to the CINCs. This process did not provide for trade-offs or for a strong institutional debate as to what was important. In part, this is attributable to the Army's focus on the retention of its FS and ES, both of which are determined outside the programming process. FS and ES are inputs to the process; once established, they receive funding priority. Figure 4.1 shows the resourcing decision model as it looked in 1995.

The DCSOPS is responsible for setting all of the Army's resourcing priorities. After the priorities were determined, the necessary supporting functional elements were allocated some percentage of Army resources. The Army program function was now dispersed among 14 resource panels. Before 1997, the Army PA&E was responsible for resourcing the directed priorities and then informing the leadership on what elements were not funded. Ideally, the VCSA and the CSA reviewed all requirements and, ultimately, the program decisions. The model could succeed only if the Army had a knowledgeable VCSA and CSA actively involved in all aspects of Army resourcing. The model also did not accommodate changes in OSD and joint decision processes.

The Army's reengineering efforts have included functional, process, and organizational change. These changes have been gradually implemented over several POM cycles to ensure that they are appropriately institutionalized. The ideal process includes re-establishment of an institutional vision and strategic planning. The strategic planning process, however, focuses on institutional responses to the operational demands being articulated by the

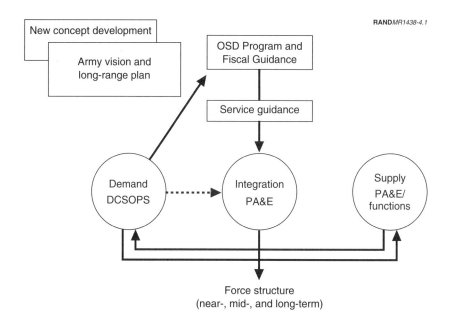

RAND*MR1438-4.1*

Figure 4.1—Army Model for Decisionmaking, 1995

CINCs and the Joint Staff rather than relying on the Army's definition of the geostrategic environment (Lewis, Brown, and Schrader, 2000). The reengineered process, developed in 1996, explicitly recognizes the joint operational demands being placed on the Services through the CINCs. In its role as a provider, the Army develops and fields capabilities to meet these demands. Development of a strong integration function is critical to balancing supply and demand. The integration function develops and assesses resource alternatives to ensure that the Army leadership is fully informed about what alternatives are available and their possible implications for the near-, mid-, and long-term Army goals and objectives identified in the Army vision and strategic plan. The Army civilian and military leaderships make program decisions from these alternatives. Figure 4.2 shows the reengineered process.

The left-hand side of Figure 4.2 shows the explicit recognition of Joint demands for Army capabilities. These are the operational demands established by the CINCs and articulated by the CJCS and the Joint Staff. The right-hand side of the figure represents the Army's institutional and, more specifically, the Title 10 functions, which include manning, equipping, and sustainment. The Title 10 functions are the supply side in that they are the mechanisms used to develop and provide Army capabilities in the near, mid-, and long terms.

Figure 4.2 also shows the addition of both a vision and a strategic planning function to the Army PPBES function. The vision provides the institutional guidance that is made operational in the strategic plan. The vision and strategic plan need to address both sets of demands being placed on the Army: the joint operational demands (left side) and the institutional demands (right side). Balance between the two demands is achieved through the strong integration function (center). The integration function provides the resource alternatives and the associated assessments that iteratively inform the leadership as to what the options are and their resource implications over time.

Ideally, the Army process seeks to develop a healthy tension between the operational and institutional demands being placed on the Army. The goal is to have maximum visibility of the important issues confronting the institution and an understanding of their potential

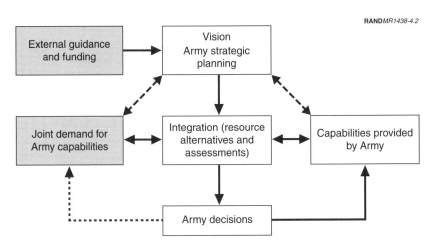

RAND*MR1438-4.2*

**Figure 4.2—Reengineered Army Strategic Planning
and Programming, 1999**

cross-functional impacts. Supporting this conceptual goal is the development of the Army mission areas and the six Program Evaluation Groups (PEGs). The Army mission areas are derived from the CINC missions that are defined in such documents as the DPG, the National Security Strategy, and the National Military Strategy. These mission areas, which change over time, focus on the aspects of missions that specifically call for Army operational capabilities (Lewis, Brown, and Schrader, 2000; Lewis, Thie, et al., 2000). For example, the Army recently added the Support to Homeland Defense mission area in recognition of the renewed interest in this area by the national security community and its discussion of the Army's role in supporting the mission.[10] Figure 4.3 shows how the mission areas and Title 10 PEGs interact in determining possible resource allocations.

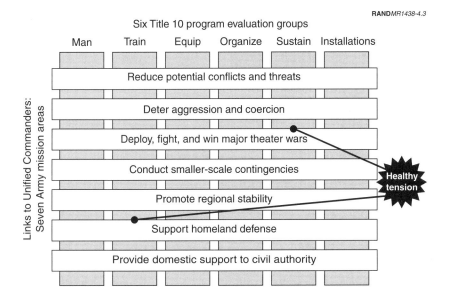

Figure 4.3—Interaction of the Mission Areas and Title 10 PEGs

---

[10]The Army National Guard is increasingly being asked to provide some level of support in this mission area, particularly in the area of responses to possible chemical and biological attacks on U.S. cities and installations. (According to Army working papers dated October 1999.)

The "healthy tension" shown in Figure 4.2 illustrates the issues on which the Army leadership might need insight. This example focuses on two current issues the Army is confronting. The first is its desire to improve its sustainment capabilities in the Major Theater War mission area, which involves shrinking the Army's logistics footprint while ensuring that its combat service and combat service support capabilities are sufficient to meet the operational demand. The second issue is that the Army's training responsibilities have increased because of the reemphasis on the Homeland Defense mission area. The Army must decide, as an institution, what type and how many resources it is going to provide to meet each of these demands. Interestingly, in the old process both of these issues would have been addressed exclusively within the Army National Guard PEG because both primarily involve the Army National Guard; the leadership would not have had visibility into how their decisions affected operational requirements in two important areas for the Army (Lewis, Brown, and Schrader, 2000).

The Army's biennial PPBES process is consistent with OSD's schedule, in which the Services produce a major POM every two years and a supporting "mini-POM" in the intervening year. A POM Update (or mini-POM) is produced annually. The ideal Army process begins with its strategic planning process and mission area assessments. Through a series of working sessions and informal exchanges, the Army Strategic Planning Guidance (ASPG) and mission area assessments determine both what the future demands on the Army are and what new concepts are needed. Both analyses are done in the context of supporting the leadership's vision of the future Army. The ASPG is published as a separate document in the spring of even-numbered years in anticipation of informing the programmers of key Army issues and their relative priority. A summary of the ASPG and the outputs of the mission area assessments are incorporated into The Army Plan. This plan, which informs the Army programmers of the program plan and is the crosswalk between planning and programming, contains three sections: Section I is the summary of the ASPG; Section II contains the outputs of the mission area assessments; and Section III contains the material that is used to give the programmers initial guidance on the Army priorities. As the Army moves toward its formal programming phase, final programming guidance to programmers is provided in a technical memorandum, which consists of a few pages and presents some last-minute guidance based on recent changes in OSD and/or Army leadership guidance.

The programming process is supported by a series of hierarchical decisionmaking bodies. All decisionmaking bodies within the Army are cochaired by members of the ARSTAF and the Secretariat. The hierarchical nature of decisionmaking within the Army attempts to ensure that at each level, appropriate issues are raised and adjudicated according to leadership guidance. Ideally, by the time the senior Army leadership reviews the process, they are addressing essential issues rather than focusing on marginal questions that have not been resolved at a lower level. This is referred to as the Planning, Programming, and Budget Committee. To support the concept of hierarchical decisionmaking and visibility across issues, the DCSPRO and Army PA&E develop scorecards identifying key Army issues (e.g., POM drivers) and develop parameters for evaluation (e.g., POM parameters). Figure 4.4 shows the ideal process and its stages.

As noted earlier, the ARSTAF attempts to involve members of the Secretariat in all aspects of decisionmaking. In part, this is a response to the Secretariat's argument that, before 1995, it had not been actively involved in essential Army decisionmaking forums. Although the Army has established new procedures and redesigned processes, the DCSOPS still predominates in decisionmaking for both planning and programming. Figure 4.5 summarizes the players involved in Army decisionmaking through each phase of the PPBES as of October 1999.

STATUS OF REENGINEERING EFFORTS

In June 1999, then-CSA GEN Eric Shinseki determined that additional reengineering and reorganization efforts were needed both to ensure better operation of the ARSTAF and to improve Army involvement and linkages to OSD and joint decisionmaking processes. General Shinseki noted that he wanted to integrate Army decisionmaking processes and to ensure that formal and informal activities supported the Army leadership in its interactions with OSD and Joint Staff decisionmaking bodies. In essence, the CSA argued for a different Army (Shinseki, 1999). Toward this end, General Shinseki directed the creation of four Army task forces: (1) vision, (2) strategic plan, (3) modernization investment, and (4) reorganization.

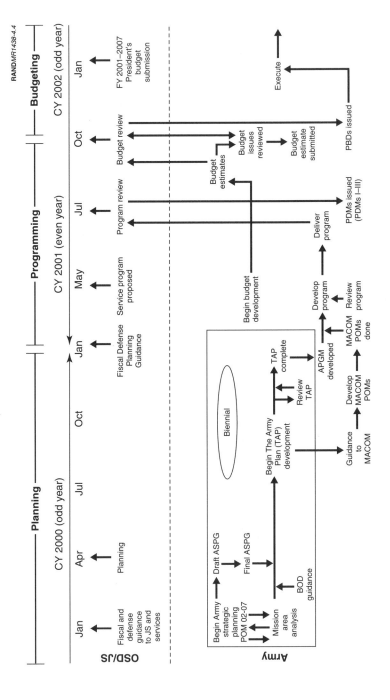

Figure 4.4—The Army PPBES Process

RAND*MR1438-4.5*

Agency	Planning	Programming	Budgeting	
OSD	USD(P)	ASD(PA&E)	DoD(C)	
JS	J5	J8	J8	
Secretariat/ ARSTAF	ARSTAF	ARSTAF	Secretariat	ARSTAF
	DCSOPS DAMO-SS DAMO-FD DAMO-OD DAMO-ZR	DCSPRO/ DCSOPS PA&E DAMO-ZR	FM&C, Army budget resource analysis	DCSOPS/ DCSPRO PA&E DAMO-ZR

SOURCES: VCSA (1999), working papers on Phase II of the reorganization dating from January–February 2000, a process improvement point paper from June 1999, and Army off-site notes and recommendations from June 1999.

Figure 4.5—Army Organizations Involved in the PPBES Process, 1999

The Army has succeeded in reinstitutionalizing its planning process but is now refocused on institutional planning rather than on the large geopolitical assessments that were done prior to 1991. The planning process, however, still tends to be too bottom-up in that the various functional planners and MACOMs provide inputs from which planning options are derived and then shared with the leadership. Eventually, one of the options is chosen and becomes the institutional plan. The senior Army leadership recognizes this problem and is attempting to remedy it by providing clear, up-front guidance through its task-force initiatives before the spring 2000 planning cycle begins. The CSA used the ASPG as the mechanism to provide guidance to the institution. In addition, the CSA has embedded his Army transformation team in the Vision and Planning Directorate within the DCSOPS organization.

In January 2001, the CSA approved an additional reorganization. The reorganization renamed the AVCSA office to DCSPRO. The DCSOPS retains all responsibilities for the prioritization of Army requirements, oversight of and responsibility for current operations and training, and operational readiness. The DCSOPS will coordinate the JCS sessions.

The DCSPRO is responsible for generating options across the totality of Army requirements and for developing and defending the Army's POM. The office provides analytic support for cross-functional issues, operates as a clearinghouse for major Army analyses, and provides the initial support for key DoD reviews. It also has oversight over the modernization portfolio.

To support the DCSPRO's functions, Army PA&E and the staff performing the PA&E and modernization functions will move out of the Office of the CSA and become part of the DCSPRO organization. Some analytic assets from the existing AVCSA and DCSOP organizations were consolidated and are now shared and jointly managed by the DCSOPS and the DCSPRO. The AVCSA office was abolished, and the three-star position was reassigned to the DCSPRO organization. The DCSPRO will be responsible for coordinating and preparing the VCSA and the CSA for all resource-related decision forums, including the DRB, JROC, JWCA, and Program Review Groups.

For this proposed reorganization to work, the Army senior leadership, particularly the VCSA, must be knowledgeable about the roles and responsibilities of the DCSOPS and DCSPRO. The VCSA will integrate supply (DCSPRO) and demand (DCSOPS) and is the individual who must demand that both the DCSOPS and the DCSPRO provide options for decisionmaking that look beyond the near term.

The Secretary of the Army and the CSA agreed that the responsibility for determining Army requirements and their prioritization needed to reside within headquarters. Since 1993, when the Army requirements process was reassigned from the headquarters to the Training and Doctrine Command, the leadership has lost its ability to link Army requirements to its planning and programming cycles and to OSD and Joint Staff processes. This detachment from the resourcing environment has damaged the Army's ability to argue for its programs and associated resources. In January 2001, the responsibility for all requirement approval was returned to the CSA.

The Army is also attempting to get more efficiency and reduce staff size by merging its acquisition and logistics functions. Collocating the acquisition and logistics functions within the acquisition function will improve the Army's ability to develop systems in which logistics functions are considered early in the design. This reorganization is still too new to assess. However, the acquisition function does not play as dominant a role in the Army as it does in the Air Force (see Chapter Six), continuing to be associated primarily with the "how to buy" function.

The organizational and functional model the Army adopted in 2000 could hinder its ability to develop and assess options. Since the DCSOPS retains FS and ES portfolios and prioritization of all resources, the DCSPRO is free to provide any options but none that make FS and ES part of the trade space without DCSOPS review and approval. The options can also be driven by the set of DCSOPS priorities, rather than simply being a variety of options that provide different ways to achieve the Army's mid- to long-term goals, which was the organization's objective.

Chapter Five

NAVY DECISIONMAKING PROCESSES

The focus of the Navy's planning and programming decisionmaking is long-term investment. The Navy leadership reorganized its head-quarters and Secretariat staffs in 1992 in response to criticisms from Congress concerning the Navy's unresponsiveness to the Goldwater-Nichols legislation. This reorganization was sweeping in that it fundamentally changed the Navy's resource decision model from decentralized planning and programming to centralized decision-making and centralized execution—although, as will be discussed later, this model has been modified (Navy, 1999b). The changes in the decision model and the ensuing reorganization necessitated that the Navy's civilian and military leadership "break the back" of the system commanders. The reorganization also eliminated the stovepiped planning and programming functions that had each platform or system sponsor identifying his own plan and resourcing.[1]

By the time the Navy undertook its reorganization in 1992, the ramifications of the Goldwater-Nichols legislation were becoming better understood. In particular, the Navy leadership recognized that any proposed reorganization had to both bring the Service into compliance with the legislation and incorporate joint decisionmaking. Particular attention had to be paid to increased involvement of the Joint Staff in resource decisionmaking. The Navy responded to these changes by organizationally and functionally aligning the Chief of Naval Operations (CNO) staff in the manner of the Joint Staff. The

---

[1]The platform sponsors were three-star admirals who oversaw the major investment programs of the Department of the Navy. Op-02 was in charge of submarines, Op–03 oversaw surface investment, and Op-05 oversaw air.

CNO's staff has a Vice Chief of Naval Operations, four Deputy Chiefs of Naval Operations, nine major staff office directors, and seven special assistants. The Marine Corps is embedded within the Department of the Navy structure and sustains a separate planning, programming, and budgeting organization.

Unlike the Army or the Air Force, the Navy's reorganization and functional realignment also considered the role of the Secretariat in the PPBS process. Although the Goldwater-Nichols legislation had moved functions to the Service Secretariats, the Navy concluded that it was important for all decisionmaking to be shared among the members of the Secretariat and CNO's staff through all PPBS phases.[2]

The Navy's centralized decisionmaking and execution model relies on a strong integration function. Figure 5.1 shows this model in 1992 before the reorganization. At this time, Integration (O90) was responsible for balancing the program after all the major decisions were made between the fleet commanders and platform sponsors.

Before the 1992 reorganization, the platform sponsors made all the important investment decisions. They were responsible both for deciding what to invest in their respective areas and for ensuring that the identified programs were sufficiently funded in the Service POM. The Navy's leadership concluded that this approach did not facilitate an integrated and balanced program, particularly during periods of declining defense expenditures. In their view, the platform sponsors had so much influence that it prevented a more integrated, corporate approach to planning and programming. In response to these internal criticisms, the Secretary of the Navy and CNO concluded that the reorganization needed to reduce the power of the individual platform sponsors and that Navy investment decisions needed to be more integrated. The platform sponsors were thus downgraded from three- to two-star admirals and were functionally and organizationally realigned to report to the newly formed Office of the Deputy Chief of Naval Operations for Resources, Warfare Requirements, and Assessments (N8), a three-star admiral. N8 is responsible for developing program investment plans and fiscally constrained investment

---

[2]As discussed in the Navy's 1992–1993 reorganization working papers.

RAND*MR1438-5.1*

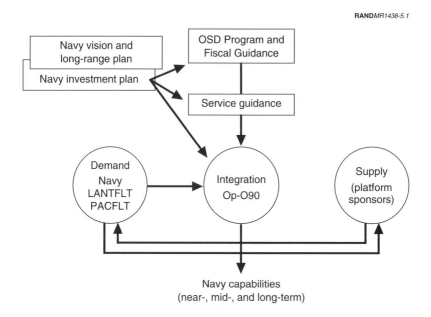

Figure 5.1—Navy Model for Decisionmaking, 1992

options and for assessing the Navy's program. He is responsible for representing the Navy in all forums and activities related to the development, presentation, and justification of the Navy's program. The organization handles all analytic efforts related to externally mandated reviews, such as the QDR.

Figure 5.2 shows the Navy's current decision model. The Navy uses a planning and programming assessment framework similar to that of the Joint Staff and that, in fact, was later modified and applied to the Joint Staff.[3] The Navy's assessment framework is divided into Joint mission areas and support areas, as shown in Figure 5.3. The framework is used to assess Navy investment plans and investment bal-

---

[3]The first N8 of the Navy, ADM William Owens, went on to become the VCJCS. The JWCAs were developed in the Joint Staff during his tenure. The assessments used the Navy model of assessing operational demands against the Title 10 functions. This is discussed in the Joint Staff's 1995–1996 working papers on JWCA formulation.

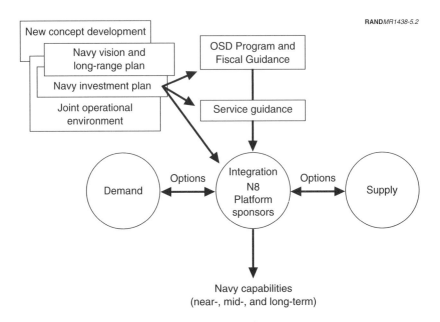

Figure 5.2—Navy Model for Decisionmaking, 1999

ance. The categories or analytic ribbons change periodically in response to changes in Navy and DoD resourcing environments and priorities. For example, two years ago, the Readiness assessment area was added because of the increased interest in readiness issues among the Joint Staff and the SECDEF. Figure 5.3 shows the Navy's current assessment framework.

Different organizations within N8 are responsible for conducting the assessments; the outputs of the assessments form the basis for generating alternatives and investment options. This approach enables the Navy to better explain its investment decisions in JROC, JRB, and DRB forums.

Strategic resource planning and programming predominate within the Navy. Institutional planning is done to ensure that the Navy is responsive to the Joint Strategic Planning System and its outputs. The Navy planning process is classic military long-range planning that includes geostrategic assessments and identification of threats.

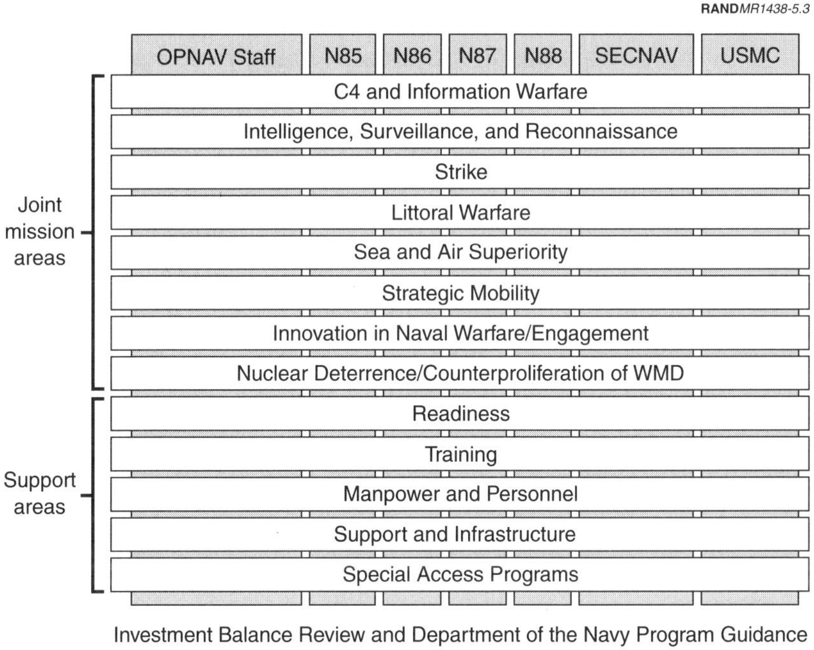

RAND*MR1438-5.3*

OPNAV Staff	N85	N86	N87	N88	SECNAV	USMC

Joint mission areas
- C4 and Information Warfare
- Intelligence, Surveillance, and Reconnaissance
- Strike
- Littoral Warfare
- Sea and Air Superiority
- Strategic Mobility
- Innovation in Naval Warfare/Engagement
- Nuclear Deterrence/Counterproliferation of WMD

Support areas
- Readiness
- Training
- Manpower and Personnel
- Support and Infrastructure
- Special Access Programs

Investment Balance Review and Department of the Navy Program Guidance

Figure 5.3—Navy Planning and Programming Assessment Framework

The outputs of the Navy planning process inform the Navy on how it should shape the Joint Strategy Review and its own investment plans. The Deputy Chief of Naval Operations for Plans, Policy, and Operations (N3/N5) oversees this process. The organization is also responsible for strategy and concepts, Navy and Joint doctrine, and current operations. The Navy long-range planning activities produce the Navy Long-Range Planning Objectives (LRPOs), a document that translates naval and Joint concepts into detailed capability requirements and support management policies. The concepts and policies also support the Marine Corps concepts. The LRPO provides guidance to the fleet CINCs and resource sponsors on how the future Navy will look and the programs it will support in subsequent POMs. The document operationalizes the Navy's vision, "Forward . . . From the Sea," and JV 2010/2020 (Navy, 1998a).

N8 is responsible for requirements, resources, and assessments and is the dominant resource organization within the Department of the Navy. It performs strategic resource planning and programming. Navy requirements are derived from the demand to demonstrate ongoing overseas presence. Strategic program planning and the development of investment options are N8's main activities.

N8 consists of approximately 400 officers and support staff. Some 20 flag and general officers are assigned to the organization and are supported by captain- and colonel-level branches. N8 is responsible for the integration of concepts, requirements, budgets, resource strategy, priorities, CINC liaison, and program and resource plans.[4] During POM development, the financial management activity is dual-supervised to ensure consistency between the programming and budgeting phases.

The assessment directorate is critical to N8's operation. Analysis and assessment capabilities are embedded in the organization to provide both quick-turnaround analyses and the ability to do longer-term investment assessments. N8, for example, oversees most externally mandated reviews both because of its linkage to Navy resources and because of the strong analytic capabilities resident within the organization. In 1998, N8 formed the Navy Planning and Strategic Planning Support cell (N81), which is now designated Assessment, to examine critical long-range strategic planning issues associated with resources. Specifically, the organization examines emerging concepts of operation that are likely to shape and influence the Department of the Navy's force levels, operations and activities, acquisition plans, and budgets over the FY 2001–2016 period. N81 is charged with preparing assessments of the impact of post–Future Years Defense Program (FYDP) options/requirements on current programs. N81 is also responsible for formulating "corporate-level" strategic programming options.[5] Figure 5.4 shows the main participants in each phase of the Department of the Navy's PPBS process.

---

[4]Like the Army, the Navy staff has recently reorganized to improve requirement definition by splitting the platform sponsors out from N8. The review process described in subsequent sections is essentially unchanged.

[5]As discussed in internal Navy working papers dated April 29, 1998.

RANDMR1438-5.4

Agency	Planning	Programming	Budgeting
OSD	USD(P)	ASD(PA&E)	DoD(C)
JS	J5	J8	J8
DON	OPA	DONPIC	FMB (NAVCOMPT)
USN	N3/N5	N8*	FMB (NAVCOMPT)
USMC	PP&O (MCCDC)	P&R	FMB (NAVCOMPT)

*Lead.

Figure 5.4—Key Participants in the Navy's PPBS Process

The Navy PPBS process is designed around OSD's PPBS schedule. Its planning phase is biennial but of shorter duration than those found in the Army and the Air Force. Integral to the program planning phase is the strategic resource-planning element; once the Navy vision and institutional plan are completed, the Navy begins a short but intense period of strategic resource planning that looks beyond the POM years.[6] The activity is part of the Integrated Warfighting Architecture Review System (IWARS). The IWARS process provides an analytic context for decisionmaking by examining Navy requirements within the context of what is desired, what currently exists, and what is planned. This process provides the CNO with an objective integrated capability and a focused understanding of current Navy plans and requirements for the future.[7] IWARS analysis includes identification of Navy objectives, tasks, and desired capabilities, which are derived from N3/N5's work on the strategy, threat, and planning guidance. The process also involves performing an end-to-end capability analysis that provides a look across the totality of Navy capabilities and, finally, an assessment of how much of a particular capability is required given current and future fiscal con-

---

[6]Like the other Services, the Navy also does a long-range program projection in response to OSD requests to review Service modernization programs and their associated costs beyond the POM years. N816B's Naval Program Projection does this (see Navy, 1998b; Navy, 1999c).

[7]According to the readiness assessment, IWARS 99, completed on May 6, 1999.

straints. The readiness assessment includes such critical areas as the flying-hour program, ship and submarine maintenance, and supply support. Other issues addressed include modernization, recapitalization, and total ownership costs.

The IWARS analysis provides input into the development of Navy-wide program options and their analytic basis. The options and their assessments are provided in the CNO's Program Analysis Memorandum, which describes the options and the course of action that the Navy will follow through the POM-development process. The IWARS process and the memorandum provide the baseline for decisionmaking through the POM process. Figure 5.5 shows the Navy's PPBS process.

Both the civilian and military leadership actively participate in a three-tiered committee process that reviews the various investment options as they emerge through the programming process. The Secretariat plays a strong role in the development and execution of the POM. It independently reviews the POM and provides recommendations to the CNO. Differences are resolved in the various decisionmaking forums in which the civilian and military leadership jointly participate.

The Department of the Navy's Program Integration Center (DONPIC) is central to the Navy's adjudication of its POM issues. This center provides integration and a baseline for decisionmaking that informs both the military and civilian leaderships of current POM decisions. The Secretary of the Navy (SECNAV) and the CNO are part of a hierarchical decisionmaking process that "establishes a framework of deliberative meetings through which significant issues to the Navy can be decided by senior Navy leaders" (CNO, 1997). These forums consist of Navy Review Boards, the Resources and Requirements Review Board, and the CNO Executive Board (CEB). Supporting these activities are CINC review boards and resource boards that include members from the Secretariat and general counsel. Special reviews are also convened as needed to address specific POM and investment issues. The Navy Secretariat is heavily involved in all phases of decisionmaking associated with development of the POM. DONPIC functions as the information center to ensure that all members of the Secretariat, as well as the SECNAV, understand where the Navy is in the POM process. DONPIC interacts and shares data

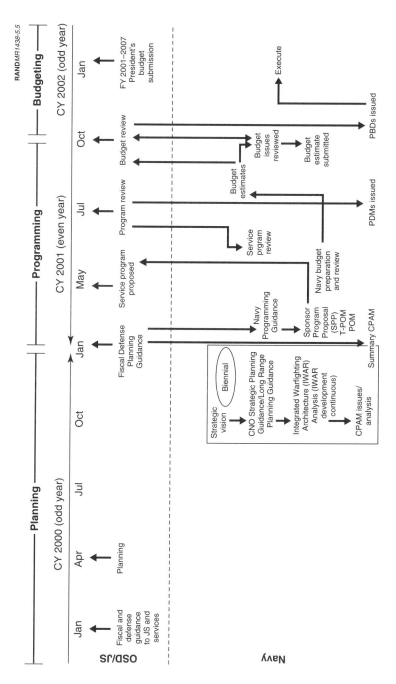

Figure 5.5—Navy Model in PPBS Process

with N8. The Navy Secretariat also independently reviews the POM and provides guidance and feedback to the CNO on major issues.

The involvement of the Secretariat is further enhanced by the dual roles that members of the Office of the Financial Management, Budget and N8 play during the programming and budgeting phase. During the programming phase, members from the comptroller's office work in N8 to ensure that budget-related issues are addressed in the programming phase. Similarly, representatives of N8 work with the staff of this office during the budgeting phase to ensure that there is minimal breakage between the programming and budgeting phases.[8] It is important to note that the U.S. Marine Corps operates within this entire structure and has separate planning and programming functions that input into the larger Department of the Navy process. The Marine Corps' positions are represented through Expeditionary Warfare Directorate (N75) within N8. The Marine Corps' budgeting activity is part of that of the total Department of the Navy, as the Goldwater-Nichols legislation directs.

ASSESSMENT AND RECENT CHANGES

The Navy leadership is generally satisfied with both the functional and the organizational alignments of the its planning, programming, and budgeting functions. All individuals interviewed insisted that the shared decisionmaking among the Secretariat, Navy, and Marine Corps is an essential element of the decision model.[9] Some individuals argue that the Navy model for decisionmaking is too centralized and that stronger and more-independent inputs are needed from the platform commanders to enhance corporate option development.[10] Some also argue that N3/N5 cannot provide a meaningful counterbalance to the dominance of N8. The model, however, is designed to make strategic program planning and investment the centerpiece of Navy planning and programming activities. The role of N3/N5 is to provide critical planning inputs to N8 and, more significantly, to represent Navy planning interests to Joint Staff and OSD planning

---

[8]According to a DONPIC memorandum dated May 6, 1999.

[9]Interviews with staff officers conducted between September 1998 and March 1999.

[10]Interview, nonattribution, November 1998.

processes. N3/N5 and N8 are aligned with Joint Staff and OSD planning and programming functions. N3/N5 is responsible for representing the Navy in the Joint Strategic Planning System process while N8 represents the Navy in J-8 activities. For example, N8 had the lead in the last QDR and is again in charge of QDR 2001.[11]

The Navy's hierarchical and shared decisionmaking structure ensures that all important resource issues are vetted at the appropriate level. The Investment Balance Review process and organization provide a critical mechanism for ensuring that controversial issues within the Navy are discussed and settled prior to any external reviews. Most of the leadership concludes that the Navy's planning, programming, and budgeting structure is responsive to the internal and external demands being placed on the Navy.

The Navy process relies on strong centralized guidance emanating from the SECNAV and CNO. N8 handles the integration function for the entire department. Its role is to provide a variety of fiscally constrained options and to allow the Service leadership to decide which course of action to pursue.

The Marine Corps planning and programming activities are handled within the Service and are then integrated into the total Department of the Navy through the N8 organization.

The Services' strong ties to the operational CINCs and the current mission demands are essential to the Navy planning and programming functions. This helps the Navy proactively shape its program while decoupling the program from the National Security Strategy and is the basis of the overseas presence argument.

In late 2000, the Navy leadership, much like that of the Army, sought to improve its requirements definition and to ensure that readiness issues were regularly addressed in the planning and programming phases. The platform sponsors were split out of N8 and were relocated in a revised N7. N7 was made a three-star position to allow requirements to compete with programs. The new position is called Deputy Chief of Operations for Requirements and Programs. N8 will now be responsible for the development of program assessments

---

[11]As discussed in J-8's kickoff workshop for Dynamic Commitment development, held June 2–3, 1999.

and budgets. The goal of the reorganization is to create a healthy tension between operational and resource issues.

Two boards will review the issues raised by the requirements and resource organizations. The first is the Executive Board, which the CNO chairs. The Executive Board sets policies and makes final decisions on how the Navy is to address its operational needs. The second review board is the Naval Requirements Oversight Council. It is responsible for reviewing and validating requests from the field. This organization is analogous to the JROC. All other functions within the Navy PPBS process remain the same.[12]

---

[12]As discussed in Navy PPBS papers dated April 2001 and in an April 2001 overview briefing on the Navy's organization.

Chapter Six

AIR FORCE REORGANIZATION, 1989–2000

The focus of Air Force decisionmaking is on investment in modernization and basing. Between the 1960s and late 1980s, the Air Force model for decisionmaking was centralized planning and decentralized execution. The Air Force headquarters decided that the Air Force's plan and program and the MAJCOMs were charged with executing the guidance. The discipline of the decisionmaking process was enforced through a strong program integration function that resided in the Air Staff. The Air Staff Program Review and Evaluation Directorate was a three-star organization that consisted of programmers whose work was supported by a strong analytic cell (Department of the Air Force, 1989). The organization had responsibility for the development and analysis of corporatewide options. The options were used to inform decisionmakers on the impacts of high-level issues confronting the Air Force. Figure 6.1 shows how the planning and programming function looked in the late 1980s. During that time, it was considered one of the most efficient and effective planning and programming organizations within DoD.

The Air Force underwent two significant reorganizations, in 1989 and 1992. These reorganizations realigned functions and processes in such a way that the decision model was fundamentally altered to evolve into consensus-built, centralized decisionmaking and decentralized execution. The preponderance of Air Force efforts during 1989 involved a reorganization focusing on the acquisition and logistics functions. In 1989, the GAO had criticized the Air Force for not being compliant with the intentions or goals of the Goldwater-Nichols legislation, contending that the institution had not

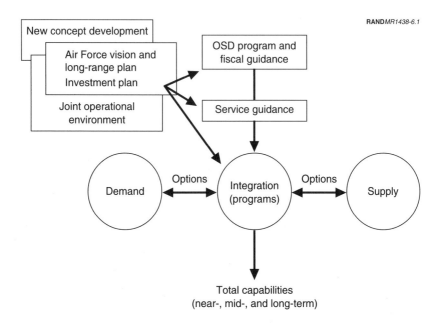

Figure 6.1—Air Force Model for Decisionmaking, 1989

fundamentally altered its organization or functions as directed by the legislation (GAO, 1989). Congress thus directed the Air Force to bring its organization and functions into alignment with the legislation.

The general philosophy adopted within the Air Force community was that authority and responsibility should be assigned to the lowest "reasonable" level. In response to this philosophy, many key Air Staff functions in both the 1989 and 1992 reorganizations were pushed to the MAJCOMs, while others were eliminated, resulting in the current model for decisionmaking (shown in Figure 6.2).[1] This model substantially weakened the integration function while strengthening the demand and supply functions. Importantly, the roles of the MAJCOMs were altered to give them direct involvement in the Air Force's PPBS process.

_____

[1]According to Air Force acquisition working papers on reorganization issues from John Welsh, Jr. from 1988 and 1989.

Dr. Donald Rice, SAF, laid out the new organizational structures in an October 2, 1989, memorandum to the SECDEF and DEPSECDEF. The Air Force sought to have centralized decisionmaking and highly decentralized execution. The memorandum noted that the corporate Air Force's organizational goals were to have a single integrated staff using the Office of Secretary of the Air Force for Acquisition (SAF[AQ]) and streamlined Air Force Space Command (AFSC) and Air Force Logistics Command (AFLC) assets to implement acquisition programs. Dr. Rice indicated that the Air Force leadership complied with the guidelines contained in DoD's DMR for the reorganization of the Air Force's acquisition function (Rice, 1989). The new reorganization was designed to push many planning and programming functions to the MAJCOMs, who were now given a much stronger voice in resource decisionmaking. The Air Force leadership saw the operational MAJCOMs as being the Air Force's direct link to the CINCs.

The 1989 acquisition reorganization concentrated on empowering the Air Force Acquisition Executive (AFAE) by establishing a three-

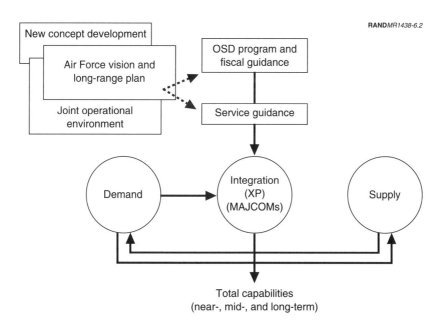

RAND*MR1438-6.2*

Figure 6.2—Air Force Model for Decisionmaking, 1999

tiered acquisition function. The AFAE's responsibilities encompassed the entire acquisition process, which spans Milestone 0 to the delivery of new systems or the significant modification of existing systems. In major programs, program management responsibility flowed directly, without intervention, from the AFAE to the PEOs to PMs. In programs that were not major, commanders in the AFSC Product Division and AFLC were responsible for program management.[2] Responsibility flowed directly from SAF(AQ) to commanders in the AFSC Product Division or AFLC Air Logistics Command.

The recommended structure, which was later adopted, placed the AFAE, PEOs, and PMs in charge of all Air Force acquisition programs. The AFSC and AFLC acquisition centers provided staff and expertise, overseeing the organizational entities responsible for the development and sustainment of a system. The acquisition function within the Air Force now has a key role in Air Force decisionmaking and resource allocation. Partly because of the institution's emphasis on modernization investment, the Air Force's acquisition function has evolved into an important organization that often operates on both the supply and demand sides. It also has most of the Air Force's discretionary funding. Therefore, the evolution of Air Force decisionmaking since 1989 cannot be discussed without addressing the acquisition function.

The other six functions identified in the Goldwater-Nichols legislation were placed within the Air Force Secretariat. The Air Force, however, found it increasingly difficult to operate its headquarters, given mandated reductions in both personnel and funding. Although the accompanying memoranda laid out what the Air Force believed were clear chains of command, the integration function between acquisition and the PPBS was not clearly delineated. It was assumed that integration among the acquisition programs would occur among the AFAE, the SAF, and the CSAF. The Air Staff would handle PPBS-related functions, and the SAF and CSAF would operate as integrators, option builders, and institutional decisionmakers. Over time, the acquisition function has assumed greater power within overall Air Force decisionmaking, with SAF(AQ) operating on both the supply and demand sides. SAF(AQ) often operates as a

---

[2]According to an Air Force memorandum from January 1990 and a series of internal briefings.

determinant of "what to buy" and "how to buy" because of its unique alignment with Air Force Materiel Command (AFMC). The organization, because of the Air Force's focus on modernization, owns most of the Air Force's discretionary funding.

The 1992 reorganization was in part the Air Force's response to OSD's reductions of Service headquarters staff and to the Air Force leadership's desire to fundamentally change how the Air Force did its planning and programming.[3] In that year, the SAF and CSAF reorganized the Air Staff because they wanted greater visibility into how options were developed that affected their decisionmaking on key issues. The initiative also responded to OSD's directed personnel cuts in each of the Services' headquarters staffs. In the reorganization, the powerful programming organization was disbanded and a smaller, reconfigured one was formed. The Air Force programmer was dropped in rank from a three-star to a two-star general, and the critical planning and programming functions went to the MAJCOMs. The Program and Evaluation Directorate was responsible for the development of fiscally constrained programming options. Part of that function was the integration and balancing of the various demands being placed on the total Air Force.

It was also determined during this period that separate commands for research and development and for logistics were no longer affordable, even after streamlining. The Air Force again attempted to reduce costs and increase efficiency through reductions in personnel and management overhead. AFSC and AFLC merged, creating AFMC, the Air Force's largest MAJCOM. At the time, AFMC absorbed approximately one-fifth of the Air Force's total personnel and managed approximately 52 percent of the Air Force's total budget.[4]

The commander of AFMC reports to AFAE for acquisition issues but reports to the CSAF on all other matters. Within the acquisition system, AFMC is in charge of translating user requirements into system concepts and performance specifications. In its acquisition function, AFMC oversees and manages the assets of the Air Force's materiel development, thus overseeing weapon system management "cradle to grave."

---

[3]According to internal Air Force working papers from 1989; see also GAO (1989), p. 30.

[4]According to Air Force reorganization working papers from 1991 and 1992.

In the new structure, the program evaluation function was to assess issues raised by the SAF and CSAF, who viewed themselves as the integrators of information from the MAJCOMs, directing the programmers on the options to be built and making the decisions. The SAF and CSAF concluded that any information they needed for decisionmaking could be obtained directly from the responsible organizations and from leaders within the Air Force rather than through a cumbersome and layered bureaucracy. The reorganization empowered the MAJCOMs, whose job was to identify operational requirements using insights into the operational environment that a close association with the component commanders yielded. The model was strong centralized decisionmaking and highly decentralized execution.[5] Figure 6.3 shows the Air Force resource allocation process in 1994.

The Air Force program planning activities were highly decentralized. The lack of a centralized integration function to assist the corporate organization in pulling the various pieces together hindered the Air Force's overall ability to generate alternative program options effectively, particularly during a period of declining defense expenditures. The left side of Figure 6.3 identifies the MAJCOMs and the Field Operating Agencies (FOAs) as having their own directorates for requirements. The Air Staff's role is to assist in the alignment of the MAJCOM's requirements as identified by their operational requirements directives and to inform the leadership of the overall requirements.

The Air Force acquisition structure is shown on the right in Figure 6.3. The output of the POM process directs the acquisition community to develop systems. The acquisition process is integral to POM deliberations because it provides important information on the "how to buy" question, while the MAJCOMs and the Air Staff deal

---

[5]According to RAND working papers on the Air Force PPBS process dating from 1979 through 1998 and collected in May 1999. In the course of doing this work, the project team assessed Air Force planning and programming from 1979 to 1998. The assessment examined major functional and organizational changes to the process. Historically, the Air Force has cycled in and out of periods in which it emphasized institutional and resource planning. For example, since 1981, it has emphasized and de-emphasized planning depending on critical funding and changes that it wanted to implement in its strategic direction.

RAND*MR1438-6.3*

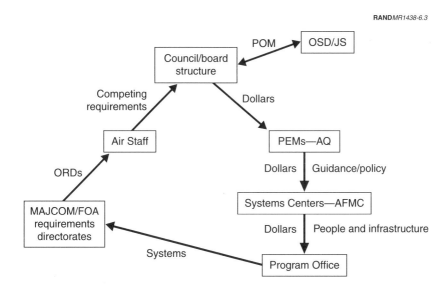

Figure 6.3—Air Force Resource Allocation Process, 1994

with the "what to buy" question. At the highest levels, the system lacks a mechanism for developing objective, integrated options and alternatives for decisionmakers. Without this capability the process could become overly focused on defining and allocating resources within the various stovepipes (i.e., the MAJCOMs and the acquisition community). This lack of a strong integration function in the planning and programming process often inhibits the Air Force from developing and executing the most efficient and effective decisions.

The goals of the 1989 and 1992 reorganizations were to create a seamless, integrated headquarters staff. The conceptual model was strong centralized decisionmaking and decentralized execution. Making this model work required a strong integration function that ensured that concepts from the field could be integrated and made consistent with the institutional vision and goals. The goal was to have a highly structured participatory system. However, the ideal model was not institutionalized; over time, many lay functions—requirements, planning, and programming—moved to the MAJCOMs, while these roles and the integration were diminished functions in the Air Staff. These activities were occurring as OSD and the Joint Staff expanded their roles in these areas. The Air Force's lack of a strong integration function at the headquarters level weakened the ability of the Service's senior leadership to conduct the business of the Air Force—which includes proactively shaping external deliberative and decisionmaking bodies—because it lacked visibility across the totality of Air Force resources.

In 1995, the revised structure did not meet the expectations of the new CSAF, Gen Ronald Fogleman. His perspective was that Air Force decisionmaking should be informed by a strong planning and program integration function, that the outputs of the corporate planning function should inform and shape MAJCOM planning, and that long-range planning should define future Air Force requirements within a joint context. The Air Force also needed to reestablish new concept development, which is a bottom-up and top-down process that seeks new ideas, both materiel and nonmateriel (Lewis, Khalilzad, and Roll, 1996).

In 1996, the council- or corporate-board structure was reestablished as part of the corporate review process to provide some capability within the Air Force to adjudicate issues within a broader participatory body. The board structure was organized around missions and mission support functions.[6] The goal was to facilitate improvements in corporate Air Force planning and programming using Integrated Process Teams in each of the panels.[7] Each of the missions and mission support panels consists of individuals who represent all the elements associated with a respective panel. This has resulted the creation of additional stovepipes through the missions and mission support activities. Since these activities were dealt with as separate stovepipes, the leadership soon realized that it had lost visibility into how decisions were reached within the mission and mission support panels. The leadership had visibility only into issues that could not be solved by the board, regardless of their relevance to the corporatewide Air Force.[8] The 1992 concept of operations was that the SAF

---

[6]According to Air Force working papers dating from 1993 to 1998, the Air Force corporate review process was restructured away from the existing 17 panels and into eight resource allocation teams based on mission areas. In 1996, the mission areas and their support functions were also adopted as the core competencies of the Air Force.

[7]The Air Force corporate structure is built around the Air Force's core competencies. These are further divided in to the missions of the Air Force and the supporting missions. See Air Force Board Structure, Air Force home page, April 2001.

[8]Interviews with Dr. Clark Murdock , June 2000, and Dr. Jake Henry, October 2000.

and CSAF could adjudicate issues raised by the MAJCOMs. MAJCOM planning and programming functions had matured in the intervening years to include the development of MAJCOM-specific plans, POMs, and funding streams. The MAJCOMs viewed these activities as best representing their interests.

The CSAF recognized that the 1989 and 1992 reorganizations were not working according to design and, in particular, that the Air Force was not doing corporate planning or programming. Its processes did not consider the joint issues and processes that were emerging within DoD. Potential joint issues and perspectives were not appropriately raised to senior Air Force decisionmakers. The acquisition function was not connected to PPBS decisions but instead operated independently. The result was that the council-board structure was not integrative, as had initially been hoped, but instead focused on POM development.

CURRENT AIR FORCE PLANNING AND PROGRAMMING ACTIVITIES

As noted earlier, General Fogleman established a single Air Staff organization in 1996 to handle the planning and programming functions. The goal was to establish an integrated planning and programming capability at the corporate level that could link Air Force planning and programming efforts and assist the Air Force in proactively shaping joint and OSD planning and resourcing activities. However, the reorganization did not address MAJCOM planning and programming activities or change the corporate-board structure. It also failed to embed within the Air Staff the ability to address joint issues in an integrated manner. For example, JROC/JWCA activities and preparing the CSAF for JCS sessions are all handled within the Office of the Deputy Chief of Staff for Air and Space Operations. These activities are not formally linked to planning and programming, although the JROC/JWCA process increasingly focuses on resource issues. Acquisition thus remains disconnected from the PPBS process, with most acquisition information coming to the programmers as information on individual systems.

The corporate Air Force's processes often attempt to mirror those found in OSD and the Joint Staff where, for instance, acquisition and the PPBS are viewed as separate but interdependent systems. The integrated staff concept has never been fully implemented, and the acquisition functions are still not relegated to the "how to buy" questions. The corporate view across stovepipes is still lacking. The re-creation of a central integrator (Headquarters, U.S. Air Force Planning and Programming [HQ USAF/XP]) was an attempt to address this latter issue, but it seems bogged down in processes that are internally focused.

Perhaps the biggest change that has come with the establishment of HQ USAF/XP has been the Air Force's development of a complex corporate strategic planning process. This biennial planning process is an attempt to provide guidance to the MAJCOMs on the major issues that face the future Air Force. The objectives of strategic planning are to sustain the Air Force's core competencies, implement the Air Force vision, integrate the headquarters and MAJCOM functional planning and programming activities, and provide analytically based options for senior leadership decisions. The planning process was initially conceived to provide a summary of the leadership's guidance and to outline the desired objectives of the Air Force over the next 10 to 15 years.

In March 1997, the first Air Force Long-Range Plan was published. This plan outlined the Air Force's vision, provided directive statements, and delineated desired end states for the Air Force for the next 25 years. In mid-1997, the Air Force Strategic Plan was conceptualized in an attempt to combine near-term performance planning with longer-term capability investment planning. This plan sought to define a framework for integrating planning and programming. By early 1998, the strategic planning process had evolved into four volumes, including detailed geostrategic assessments (Volume 1) and detailed transformation plans for the Air Force (Volume 3).[9]

The foundation of Air Force resource decisionmaking is the core competencies—Aerospace Superiority, Global Attack/Precision Engagement, Global Mobility, Agile Combat Support, and Informa-

---

[9]U.S. Air Force (1999). The four planning volumes are Volume 1: The Future Security Environment; Volume 2: Air Force Performance Plan, which establishes goals, headquarters essential tasks, performance measures, and standards; and Volumes 3 and 4 provide direction for future Air Force capability development, identify the science and technology agenda, and provide the transformation path methodology. Volumes 3 and 4 were later merged into the Long-Range Planning Guidance, which identifies key initiatives and senior-level decisions. Air Force planning documents provide further information.

tion Superiority—on which the Service bases all its program decisions.[10] Each MAJCOM is responsible for a particular competency; for example, the Air Combat Command (ACC) oversees most activities associated with the Air and Space Superiority core competency; Global Mobility is almost the exclusive domain of the Air Mobility Command; and AFMC and the Air Education and Training Command (AETC) manage the Agile Combat Support competency. The support missions—innovation, people, and quality of life—are areas the Air Force considers critical to its ability to perform its core competencies and missions (see Lewis, Pirnie, et al., 1999).

Figure 6.4 shows how the core competencies are aligned within the corporate-board structure. The board structure reviews all MAJCOM POMs and makes decisions about the overall Air Force POM. The final decisions on the hardest questions supposedly reside with the SAF and CSAF. The board structure at the one-, two-, and three-star levels adjudicates each critical issue. The corporate structure is a bottom-up process in that it starts at the lowest level with action officers reviewing and commenting on the MAJCOM POMs. Ultimately, the four-stars review the POM and decide what the final submittal to OSD will contain.[11] Figure 6.5 shows the planning, programming, and budgeting time lines within the Air Force.

Although the strategic planning process is quite complex and lengthy, it has yet to significantly alter program decisions. This is attributable in part to the complexity of the process and to the continued dominance of the MAJCOMs in shaping the Air Force agenda. The present Air Force planning and programming structure is focused on materiel solutions that are in response to a particular MAJCOM's mission area. The Air Force mission areas are not defined from a joint perspective but are instead derived from the

---

[10]The Air Force contends that the core competencies form the basis of all Air Force missions and activities. Others have argued that using the core competencies for planning purposes ignores the fact that Air Force capabilities need to be assessed within the context of joint operations. In this view, using the competencies as the basis of decisionmaking ignores the joint environment and strengthens MAJCOM determination of the Air Force capabilities because the competencies are assigned to the individual MAJCOMs. (See Lewis, Pirnie, et al., 1999.)

[11]This was explained in the Headquarters, USAF basic course on the PPBS in spring 2001.

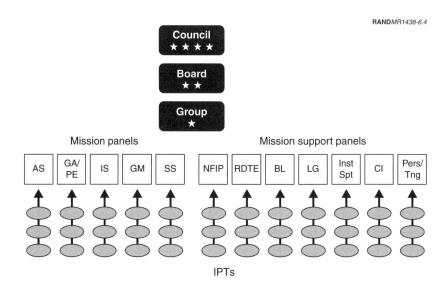

Figure 6.4—Air Force Mission and Mission Support Panels

core competencies. The missions of the Air Force are taken from the institution's core competencies. The MAJCOMs' priorities are adjudicated through the corporate-board structure, which is chaired and populated by representatives from the MAJCOMs.

ASSESSMENT AND UPDATE

The Air Force's present structure continues to be focused on materiel solutions. MAJCOM planning processes focus on the near term; they respond to programmatic guidance. This focus is understandable; the MAJCOMs' charter directs them to concentrate on CINC requirements, which have a timeline of approximately two to five years. Many MAJCOMs have established planning organizations that look past the current POM and FYDP. The difficulty, however, is that, as the provider of resources to the components, the MAJCOM often bases its decisions on current operational demands.

Given this arrangement, the dilemma for the Air Force is that its critical planning and resource identification processes are within the

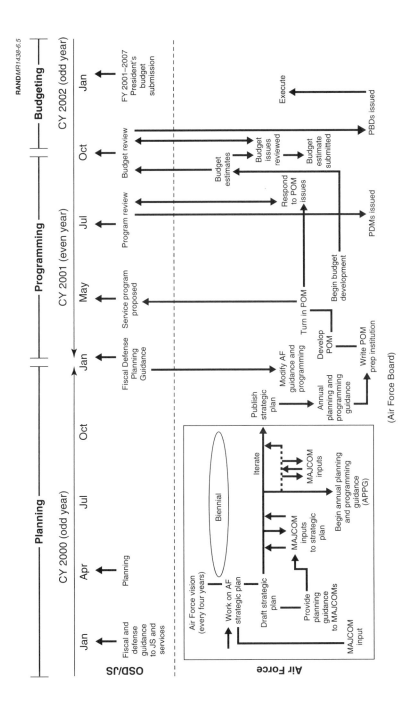

Figure 6.5—Air Force Planning, Programmin and Budgeting Process

MAJCOMs. This often prevents HQ USAF from having a lot of functional and organizational capability to implement its corporate vision, long-range plans, and new concept development over extended periods. On occasion, the Air Staff and MAJCOMs operate independently from one another.[12]

Elucidating the independence of the MAJCOMs in identifying and setting the Air Force's resourcing priorities requires some discussion of the mission-functional area planning process. Each MAJCOM conducts mission planning and sets the associated resource priorities for its particular mission area. The resource priorities are the inputs to the Mission and Mission Support panels. Because of these responsibilities, the long-range planning function really occurs within each of the mission-functional area plans.

Modernization planning has been strengthened within the MAJCOMs by increasing their oversight of the identification and setting of priorities of the fiscally constrained requirements. The value of this process is measured by an increase across the Air Force of MNSs, which are also viewed as strengthening the linkage between planning and programming because they set future requirements (planning) that must be resourced (programming).

---

[12]In 1997, the Air Force established the Battlelab concept in an attempt to take advantage of the rapid pace of technology by exploring new ideas and fostering innovative technologies that will improve the Air Force. The initial concept was to enable the Air Force to use existing technologies to facilitate innovation and revolutionary operations and logistics concepts. The concept is to experiment with and incorporate technologies into areas in which they can assist in the improvement of Air Force capabilities at a relatively low cost. The Battlelab concept would provide opportunities to reach investment decisions more quickly and to underpin the Service's Title 10 responsibilities to organize, equip, and program more effectively. Six Battlelabs have been established; oversight has been given to the HQ USAF Directorate for Space and Air Operations. The Battlelabs are funded with operation and maintenance and procurement appropriations. The dilemma for the Air Force is that, in the execution of the Battlelab concept, the labs were allocated to the MAJCOMs. Rather than have concept development driven from the top as initially conceptualized, it is now owned by the MAJCOMs and the acquisition community. The alignment of the Battlelabs with and the growing dependence on the MAJCOMs, AFMC, and acquisition almost preclude achievement of the four fundamental principles of the Battlelab concept: lean, unique, focused, and innovative. The current emphasis is on near-term fixes that could constrain the impetus for new concepts or innovation. The Battlelabs have thus far concentrated on the institutionalization of the concept, with most initiatives being limited in scope and application. (See Air Force, 1997.)

Figure 6.6 illustrates the typical MAJCOM mission planning process, which focuses on identifying requirements. The output is an array of validated requirements, many of which will be funded. The modernization plan is also an attempt to provide the Air Force leadership a look out at the next 25 years. The predicament of this approach, however, is that the mission areas, from which the requirements are identified, are internal to the Air Force.[13]

Using a stovepiped modernization process as the critical long-range planning activity for the Air Force precludes the implementation of a long-range planning function that looks across the Air Force to define future capabilities from a corporate and joint perspective. The MAJCOMs are quite pleased with this process, for it enables them to determine both the requirements and their resource priority.

The highly decentralized nature of the planning and execution activities within the Air Force suggests that institutionalizing centralized

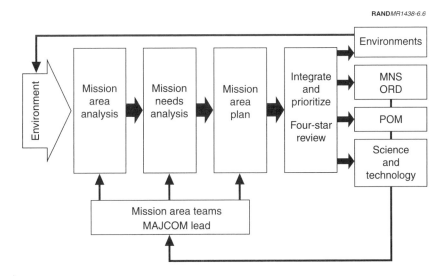

RAND*MR1438-6.6*

Figure 6.6—Air Force Mission Planning Process—Ideal Structure

---

[13]Since 1994, in response to the MAJCOMs' complaint concerning how Air Force–wide priorities were established, fiscal constraints were added to the process in an effort to make the process more relevant.

long-range planning and enhancing new concept development may require some functional and organizational realignments. Our analysis suggests that the MAJCOMs function as both demanders and suppliers of capabilities for the Air Force. In most cases, however, current operational demands predominate. The autonomy of the MAJCOMs is buttressed through their ownership of the program elements and the budgets associated with a particular program. In the current functional alignment, HQ USAF/XP lacks the charter, resources, and analytic capabilities to offset MAJCOM predominance. The current management model requires the SAF and CSAF to be strongly and consistently involved in all phases of the PPBS to provide the appropriate guidance, integration, and option development. Often the high demands being placed on the SAF's and the CSAF's time prohibit them from performing this function as it was envisioned in the 1989 and 1992 reorganizations.

The current planning and programming structure within the Air Force also does not take into full account the increased role of the CJCS and the Joint Staff in resource decisionmaking. The Air Force model is focused on the identification of requirements that are most closely aligned with the components and the CINCs. The dilemma is that these demands are now most often focused on current operations, preventing the Air Force from thinking about the longer term. Joint Staff processes now directly affect resource decisionmaking. Increasingly, the Services are required to provide solutions to long-term problems. Changes in the resource dynamics within the CJCS and OSD might necessitate that the Air Force rethink its highly decentralized approach to both planning and programming. This assessment should also include the relevance and impact of the current corporate planning process on Air Force decisionmaking.

The MAJCOM planning processes are built around mission areas that are not always compatible with the complex, centralized planning function HQ USAF/XP envisions. Rather, the current decisionmaking model suggests that, at best, the strategic plan should provide general guidance to the MAJCOMs so that they can conduct detailed mission area analysis. Current practices, however, do suggest that a strengthened integration function within the programming area would be consistent with the board structure now in place. Many individuals in the Air Force agree that a strengthened programming integration function supported by comprehensive analytic tools—

cost models, FS, and modernization databases—could increase the corporate Air Force's ability to build comprehensive options for assessment throughout the programming phase. This capability could also inform senior decisionmakers about critical issues associated with particular decisions.

The recommendation to simplify the planning and programming process does not suggest that the Air Force should abolish the process. Corporate strategic planning is critical to the institution and necessary. It should provide the top-level guidance to the institution about corporate goals and objectives and their relative priorities. The guidance, however, need not be complex and all-encompassing; rather, it needs to focus on the critical areas that the corporate Air Force considers essential to its mid- and long-term development.

AIR FORCE RESOURCE ALLOCATION PROCESS

The SAF and CSAF concluded in early 1999 that the Air Force headquarters needed to be better organized and aligned, which led to the Headquarters Air Force 2002 (HAF02) initiative. The goals of the initiative are to streamline functions, to improve the Air Force's alignment with OSD and Joint Staff processes, and to satisfy the congressionally mandated reductions in headquarters staff.[14] The initiative involves both the Secretariat and Air Staff. Several integrated business teams were formed to support the initiative; they are examining such areas as the requirements process, acquisition, modernization planning and support, and administrative functions. These teams began reporting their findings and recommendations for change during winter 1999–2000. Another HAF02 activity is an assessment of the PPBS functions. This activity is known as the Air Force Resource Allocation Process (AFRAP). In fall 2000, the AFRAP was presented for leadership review (Hogan, 2000). The process did not alter the roles and authority of the MAJCOMs and continues to emphasize modernization. The revised process does, however, imply a stronger role for the Air Staff and, in particular, the Planning and Programming Directorate to be more integrative and to develop

---

[14]Congress has imposed a number of personnel reductions on DoD since 1995. The directed headquarters reductions mandated a 35-percent reduction between 1996 and 1999. The 1999 congressional language directed additional reductions of 21 percent of the 1999 baseline. (National Defense Authorization Act for Fiscal Year 2000.)

alternatives for senior leadership review. The AFRAP concept proposes a four-step process:

1. Determine capability objectives
2. Develop capability options
3. Allocate resources
4. Execute resources and assess performance.

Analysis forms the linchpin of the AFRAP concept. The goal is to reestablish and maintain a broad set of analytic tools at the MAJCOMs as well as at the headquarters (AFRAP Team, 2001).

In late 2000, the Air Force leadership adopted the AFRAP and directed that it be implemented. Key to the implementation of AFRAP is the development of a capabilities construct. AFRAP implementation has been held up because the senior leadership cannot decide which should be the fundamental organizing element for the construct, core competencies, or capabilities. The current trend is to base the construct around core competencies and the 14 current future capabilities, which are identified in Volume 3 of the strategic plan (Barry, 2001b). Several draft constructs have gone forward to the leadership that proposed a combination of capabilities and core competencies (Barry, 2001a). In addition, the Air Force has also developed a construct focused on mission areas; this is called Concepts of Operation (CONOPS) 2020.

In fall 2000, the Air Force leadership decided to conduct a programming experiment in its off-year POM process, which is called APOM 03. The APOM 03 experiment further empowers the MAJCOMs in that they are now allocated dollar thresholds. The corporate Air Force withheld marginal dollars; in prior years, the corporate withhold covered a multitude of bills that the MAJCOMs would or could pay. The experiment calls for the MAJCOMs to develop and execute their own programs within their allocated top lines. The guidance to the MAJCOMs was contained in the Air Force Planning and Programming Guidance (APPG), which was negotiated between the Air Staff and MAJCOMs prior to its approval and issuance in November 2000.[15]

---

[15]According to APOM working papers of February 2001 and the APPG of November 2000.

The initial MAJCOM APOM briefings went through panel review. The MAJCOMs rejected paying many bills associated with sustainment and other nonmodernization bills.[16] The APOM deliberations were suspended pending the outcome of DoD's strategic review, which began in February 2001. Recently, the Air Force leadership decided to build its 03 POM around the mission areas described in CONOPS 2020. The Air Force is attempting to reconcile its funding shortfalls with the increases in operational demands through the direct association of resources with CONOPS 2020 mission areas. As of this writing, the 03 POMs continue to be developed.

The Air Force is still grappling with the AFRAP construct and how it might be implemented. The leadership has not determined how it will manage the relationship between the headquarters and the MAJCOMs after implementation of a construct. There are indications that MAJCOM planning and programming responsibilities will increase as headquarters attempts to meet reductions Congress has directed for the staffs of Service headquarters. In the meantime, the leadership is also attempting to strengthen the integration function by developing and implementing the capabilities construct. The corporate structure will continue to be the dominant body for adjudicating and making Air Force–wide decisions. There is little question, however, that a construct will be implemented, but how it will be managed and its exact structure are still being debated.

---

[16]According to APOM panel briefings held February 7–9, 2001.

Chapter Seven

SUMMARY, CONCLUSIONS, AND RECOMMENDATIONS

This assessment of changes in Service planning and programming functions since the passage of the Goldwater-Nichols legislation in 1986 has provided several insights. The involvement of the Joint Staff in resource decisionmaking has exceeded what the designers of the legislation envisioned.[1] In part, this has been in response to changes in the geostrategic environment. Designed in the waning years of the Cold War, the legislation reflects the Cold War emphasis on the forces and weaponry to fight a large-scale war with the Soviet Union. The idea was to counterbalance the Services' dominant role in determining forces and weaponry with that of the CINCs and the CJCS. Because the legislation focused on a relatively stable threat environment, it was not designed to operate in the complex, multiple-contingency environment in which DoD operates today.

Jointness within the context of Goldwater-Nichols legislation means the achievement of the best mix of resources to provide the most effective and efficient capabilities to meet operational demands. Declines in defense expenditures since the mid-1980s, combined with the increase in operations, has sometimes emphasized integration of capabilities. Integration in this context means the combination of resources to provide a set of cost-effective capabilities.[2] Today the Joint Staff is increasingly involved in all aspects of operational and resource decisionmaking. Many would argue that this is

---

[1]Interviews with congressional staff involved in drafting legislation, September 1998.

[2]Archie D. Barrett, congressional staff interviews, September 1998.

an unanticipated by-product of the Goldwater-Nichols legislation. Some further contend that it is a natural outgrowth of involving the CINCs and CJCS in resource decisionmaking as designated by the Goldwater-Nichols legislation.

Currently OSD and the Joint Staff have yet to fully resolve where each other's functional responsibilities rest. The 1996–1997 QDR revealed strikingly different perspectives between the two organizations concerning their roles and responsibilities. During the summer of 1996, when preparations were under way for the QDR, both OSD and the Joint Staff contended that the process would be comanaged. For a variety of reasons, the Joint Staff managed the early phases of the QDR. During the course of the QDR, the JROC assumed the role as the organization to vet QDR-wide issues. In the concluding days of the review, the SECDEF brokered the final agreements by working directly with the CJCS and the Service chiefs (Schrader, Lewis, Brown, 1999; Thomason et al., 1998). In part, this arrangement evolved because the services distrusted both the Joint Staff and OSD. Recent attempts to address readiness issues also illuminate the fact that the functional responsibilities of OSD and the Joint Staff have yet to be fully resolved.[3] Current QDR 2001 efforts reflect the many ambiguities over responsibility that have not been resolved.[4]

The disunity of the Joint Staff and OSD provides opportunities for the Services to influence all aspects of DoD decisionmaking. Doing this, however, requires that the Services be keenly attuned to all aspects of OSD and Joint Staff activities that could affect them and have well-defined and efficient planning, programming, and budgeting functions. The Services need to ensure that their military and civilian

---

[3]OSD would argue that it has policy oversight within DoD and provides the direction and guidance for the Services. On the other hand, given the weight that operational issues have had in decisionmaking and the dominance of the CINCs in articulating to Congress their demands for resources given the increase in operations, the CJCS—and therefore, the Joint Staff—is playing an increasing role in defining resource requirements. This role has been further strengthened by the focus on operational readiness, which has been linked to resources.

[4]As of this writing, the Joint Staff is preparing for QDR 2001. The key members of OSD are political appointees and are therefore waiting for the next administration to handle preparation and management of the next QDR. However, several career civilians within OSD are performing some important functions such as strategic planning and model analyses. This is discussed in Joint Staff and OSD working papers on QDR 2001, September 2000 to March 2001.

staffs are operating in concert so that they represent a single, well-articulated viewpoint to external decisionmaking bodies.

In the end, there is no perfect decision model. The models the Services use reflect their institutional focus. The centralized decisionmaking, decentralized execution decision model supports the Army's focus on retention of FS and ES. The decision model supports using FS and ES as inputs to both the planning and programming phases of the PPBS. Processes that operate outside the formal PPBS system determine the FS and ES; the headquarters determines the sizes of the FS and ES and how they will be funded. It is the job of the MACOMs to execute the decisions (e.g., decentralized execution). The activities associated with POM building concentrate on attaining some investment balance in other program areas while sustaining the predetermined FS and ES—logistics, modernization, intelligence, etc.

In recent years, affordability issues and the Army's inability to justify its resource priorities to OSD, the Joint Staff, and Congress have encouraged the leadership to reengineer its planning and programming functions. Importantly, the Army's reengineering efforts seek to provide the leadership greater visibility into the totality of its resources and the development of options. The reengineering efforts do not, however, address changing the resource decision model.

The Navy changed its resource decision model in the early 1990s. It moved from a decentralized decision model to a highly centralized model. Critical to the implementation of the new decision model was redefining the role of the platform sponsors. The power and independence of the platform sponsors, who controlled all big investment decisions, was restricted. They were downgraded in rank from three to two stars and were directed to work for the newly empowered N8 organization. The changes in the decision model necessitated changing existing processes and establishing new ones. For example, the Navy strengthened DONPIC's role to ensure that the Secretariat was involved in all phases of program decisionmaking and created additional hierarchical review boards in both the secretariat and Navy staff. The Navy also anticipated the increased role the CINCs and CJCS would play in resource decisionmaking. The Navy staff was realigned to ensure that it could respond to the various staff and forums emerging within the Joint Staff. In the early 1990s, the Navy decoupled its resource justification from the threat and redefined its resource requirements according to the concept of overseas presence.[5] This resource strategy served the institution well during the 1990s (Navy, 1999a).

The Air Force focuses on investment in modernization and basing, and this dominates its planning and resource decisionmaking. The Air Force resource decision model changed in the early 1990s, although this was not the goal of either the SAF or CSAF. Rather, the SAF and CSAF sought to increase the participation of the MAJCOMs by empowering them to provide inputs to the headquarters on requirements. The CSAF and SAF wanted to function as the option developers and ultimate decisionmakers. To do so, they reduced the authority and responsibility of the programming organization by reducing the power of the programming organization through staff reductions and reducing the rank of the director from a three- to a two-star general.

The rationale for the reorganization was to reduce the size of the headquarters staff and to strengthen the Air Force's link to the joint operational community through the MAJCOMs and components. The SAF and CSAF viewed themselves as the resource integrators, option developers, and ultimate decisionmakers. The programming organization was responsible for developing directed options.

Conceptually, this decision model adheres to the construct of supply, demand, and integration. The operational MAJCOMs—such as ACC, AMC, and Space Command—set the demand, while the supporting commands—such as AFMC and AETC—and the functional groups constitute the supply. The SAF and CSAF perform integration. The problem is that, if the SAF and CSAF do not participate actively in the integration and option-development activities, the model cannot operate as intended. In addition, directed personnel reductions in the headquarters resulted in the transfer of many essential functions—planning, option development, and priority setting—to the MAJCOMs. Thus, the MAJCOMs operate on both the supply and

---

[5]The overseas presence argument is that the Navy is sized to meet CINC demands on the basis of the requirement to provide a presence around the world regardless of MTWs or contingencies. The overseas presence requirement sizes the requirement for the number of carrier battle groups, which consist of a certain minimum combination of air, surface, and below-surface assets. In the case of contingencies or a major theater war, the assets are tailored and reallocated based on the operational demands.

demand sides. The acquisition function is in a unique position within this structure. The merging of acquisition with logistics and the creation of AFMC have given acquisition a predominant role in determining both what the Service buys and how it buys it. The acquisition function has discretion over a great deal of funding within the Air Force. Its predominance is not challenged because of the emphasis the institution places on modernization and base support.

This model worked as long as the CSAF and SAF played a dominant, everyday role in planning and programming. However, continued downsizing of headquarters staff and changes in leadership have pushed the desired model more toward consensus-built, centralized-decentralized decisionmaking, with decentralized execution. Conceptually, the Air Force model of centralized decisionmaking and decentralized execution, supported by a well-structured participatory process, is not bad. The dilemma is that, for the model to work as envisioned, the SAF and CSAF must be knowledgeable and actively involved in all phases of planning, programming, and budgeting—and this has not been the case since the reforms were implemented.

If the Air Force wants to adhere to its decision model, it is necessary to strengthen the programming integration function. The Air Force leadership took some steps in this direction in 1996 and 1997 by combining planning and programming and putting a three-star general in charge. The difficulty has been that the reorganization stopped short of officially reempowering the programmer with the authority to examine MAJCOM requirements and to develop broad institutional options. The reorganization also stopped short of addressing the fundamental relationship between the MAJCOMs and the Air Staff. For example, in a period of increased centralized resource decisionmaking by the Joint Staff and OSD, is it efficient to have the MAJCOMs develop their own POMs and own their own program elements and funding streams? If the Air Force were to increase the responsibilities of its Directorate of Programs (the programming organization), could the MAJCOMs continue to operate in the same manner?

Recent reengineering initiatives are designed to specifically address some of these problems. The holistic, integrated approach directed by the SAF and CSAF is promising. The key, however, is to develop and implement changes that are good for the total institution and not the result of consensus-developed recommendations.

Some general conclusions can also be drawn from this assessment. The Services have been slow to understand the implications of increased jointness on their decisionmaking authority and associated processes. The Navy has been the most proactive in understanding the potential implications of jointness on its resource decisionmaking processes. Its reorganization and process reengineering was done in part to be responsive to emerging joint processes and the operation of the Joint Staff. The Army and the Air Force responded to functional changes in the Joint Staff that implementation of the Goldwater-Nichols legislation brought on by adding to existing processes. Any realignment of organizational responsibilities was in direct response to the directives laid out in the legislation. The Army is currently rethinking aspects of its organizational and functional alignments as one way to improve internal decisionmaking and to be more responsive to changes in OSD and Joint Staff decisionmaking. The Air Force has expressed some dissatisfaction with its resourcing processes, particularly in the development of corporatewide options. Reorganizations and process reengineering are difficult for all the Services because they must respond to a 25-percent congressionally mandated headquarters workforce reduction by 2002 at the same time they face recruitment and retention problems.

This assessment has attempted to sketch how the various Services are currently performing their planning and programming functions. It is important to recognize these issues in a period in which the military departments are being judged, rightly or wrongly, as too parochial and entrenched to adopt joint concepts and develop systems that support joint operational capabilities.

Secretariat involvement in resource decisionmaking also differs among the Services. Civilian participation in Service decisionmaking often depends on personality. Secretaries and undersecretaries who wish to be involved usually become enmeshed in the process; otherwise, the military leadership oversees most of the activities just as it did before the passage of the Goldwater-Nichols legislation. Currently, the Navy has the most Secretariat involvement in its planning, programming, and budgeting activities. The Army Secretariat has increased its participation since 1993 by demanding that all Army planning and programming activities include its representatives. Most panels and decisionmaking bodies are cochaired by a member from the Secretariat and ARSTAF.

All the Services have attempted to deal with the emergence of cross-functional issues through the development of an integration function. The integration function also provides the linkage to the resources. Within the Army, the integration function is just emerging with the establishment of the AVCSA office and, more recently, with the implementation of the DCSPRO organization. The goal is to develop a capability that can integrate cross-functional issues and link the issues to resources. The DCSPRO would also be responsible for the development of options and for managing externally mandated reviews, such as the QDR. The problem for the DCSPRO in option development is that he does not determine FS and ES, which are still owned and managed by the DCSOPS.

The Navy has the most established integration function through the N8 organization, which provides investment options to the Navy leadership and oversees critical reviews. N8 also has a strong analytic capability that provides institutional continuity for both investment and the representation of Navy investment interests to outside organizations. Individuals inside and outside of the Navy have leveled criticisms against the N8 organization, contending that the organization is too strong and that its dominance prohibits sharing viewpoints from the field throughout the institution. Some critics further maintain that N8 only continues Navy parochialism because of the organization's predominant role in all Navy decisionmaking. (A recent reorganization has reduced the predominance of N8, retaining most of the benefits of the earlier centralization.)

Before 1992, the Air Force had a powerful integration office with the Program and Evaluation organization. Well-trained staff supported by strong analytics provided the Air Force leadership with near-, mid-, and long-term investment options. Most of these capabilities were abandoned with the 1992 reorganization. The institution has come to rely on the MAJCOMs to provide the options in the areas for which they were responsible. The recreation of the board structure in 1997 has not overcome the absence of a strong corporate integration capability because the body is not supported by a strong analytic function. The new programming organization—the Air Force Directorate of Programs—lacks the authority to develop corporatewide options, as well as the analytic capability that existed before 1992. Rather, its focus is on developing options within the narrow confines of a particular issue in support of the board. The Air Force leadership is well aware of the need to develop a strong integration function but is unwilling to do so within the context of addressing the relationship between the headquarters and MAJCOMs in terms of defining mid- and long-term Air Force requirements and setting their priorities. To do this, the Air Force leadership would have to decide that it wants this type of capability reestablished and would then have to support it.

This assessment has borne out the contention that the complexities the passage of the Goldwater-Nichols legislation introduced into DoD, followed closely by the collapse of the Soviet Union, have necessitated changes in both Service perspectives and functions. The Services' military leadership dominated decisionmaking in all areas before 1986, determining what the requirements were and how they would be resourced over time. The goal of the legislation was to curtail some of the Services' dominance in all areas of resourcing by involving both the CJCS and the CINCs. The collapse of the Soviet Union and the demise of the bipolar world have caused significant instability in Africa, Latin America, and Eastern Europe. The associated social, economic, and political realities have resulted in more-extensive use of the U.S. military for a variety of missions—humanitarian operations, peacekeeping, etc.—none of which approach a major theater war in scope or military demand for which most service planning is focused. This analysis supports the findings of other scholars that large bureaucracies change slowly. Large bureaucracies are risk-averse and attempt to manage risk by avoiding large-scale changes. In some respects, DoD has been slow to respond to the Goldwater-Nichols legislation and to changes in the geopolitical environment.

On the other hand, there has been little external pressure on DoD to make its operations more efficient. The recent legislation to further reduce OSD and Service staff headquarters has met with strong resistance inside the Pentagon. The Services argue that further reductions will hinder their ability to perform basic processes while still providing sufficient manpower to meet current operational demands. The Services in general have not undertaken a drastic second look at functions they perform in their respective headquarters.

For the most part, all the Services continue to perform most of the pre–Goldwater-Nichols legislation functions that support their decision processes and have added on such functions as supporting the JWCA/JROC process. The underlying assumption for most of the Services has been just to assign more duties to the civilian and military workforces, basically viewing them as a free commodity. The concepts of efficiency and effectiveness have not been applied. No quantitative studies show how much the workload within the Pentagon has increased for the average worker since the passage of the Goldwater-Nichols legislation and the collapse of the Soviet Union.

In conclusion, this assessment of Service decisionmaking processes has shown that the processes reflect the cultures of the individual institutions and that change has been slow and often not strategically directed. The military departments are only now addressing the continued expansion of jointness, which the individual departments do not always view as useful but rather a challenge to Service-perceived prerogatives.

AFRAP Team—*See* Air Force Resource Allocation Process Team.

Air Force Resource Allocation Process Team, "AFRAP Process Design," briefing, January 2001.

Army—*See* U.S. Army.

Barry, John, AF(XPX), "AFRAP Implementation," briefing, February 22, 2001a.

_____, Rosetta Stone briefing, April 2001b.

Blumenfeld Panel, "Report on Blumenfeld Panel Review of the Army's Senior Level Decision Making Process," Final Draft, May 2, 1995.

Chairman of the Joint Chiefs of Staff, *Chairman's Program Review*, May 1997a.

_____, "Joint Strategic Planning System," Washington, D.C., Instruction 3100.01, September 1, 1997b.

_____, *Chairman's Program Review*, May 1998.

_____, "Chairman of the Joint Chiefs of Staff, Commanders in Chief of the Combatant Command, and Joint Staff Participation in the PPBS," Washington, D.C., Instruction 8501.01, April 1, 1999a.

_____, "The Joint Wafighting Capabilities Assessment Process," Washington, D.C., Instruction 3137.01, January 22, 1999b.

_____, "Charter of the Joint Requirements Oversight Council," Washington, D.C., Instruction 5123.01, March 8, 2001.

_____, JROC Charter, J-8, draft, October 1999.

CJCS—*See* Chairman of the Joint Chiefs of Staff.

CNO—*See* Office of the Chief of Naval Operations.

Defense Authorization Act of 1996, Public Law 104-106, February 10, 1996.

DoD—*See* U.S. Department of Defense.

Department of the Air Force, Office of the General Counsel, memorandum, March 24, 1987.

_____, *Air Force Organizations and Functions: 1949–1988*, Vols. 1 and 2, 1989.

Department of the Navy, *Navy Budget Highlights Book*, February 1999a.

_____, "Navy Long-Range Planning Objectives," briefing, March 1998b.

_____, N816B, "Naval Program Projection Overview Briefing," May 4, 1998c.

_____, "Navy PPBS: A Macro Process Perspective, Block II," briefing, May 1999a.

_____, "Navy Programming," briefing, July 1999b.

_____, "Navy Organization: An Overview," April 2001.

Eash, Joseph J., III, "Advanced Technology Demos Empower Warfighters with Tomorrow's Weapons," *National Defense*, July/August 1998.

GAO—*See* U.S. General Accounting Office.

Goldwater-Nichols—*See* Goldwater-Nichols Department of Defense Reorganization Act of 1986.

Goldwater-Nichols Department of Defense Reorganization Act of 1986, Public Law 99-433, October 1, 1986

Hewes, James E., Jr., *From Root to McNamara: Army Organization and Administration 1900–1963*, U.S. Army Center of Military History, Washington, D.C., 1975.

Hogan, Dan, AF(XP), "The AFRAP Process," December 2000.

Joulwan, George, CINCEUR, letter to the Secretary of Defense and the Chairman of the Joint Chiefs of Staff, April 15, 1995.

Thomason, James S., Paul H. Richanbach, Sharon M. Fiore, Deboarh P. Christie, *Quadrennial Review Process: Lessons Learned form 1997 Review and Options for the Future*, Alexandria, Va.: Institute for Defense Analyses, P-3402, August 1998.

"Joint Forces Command Assumes Future Area of Responsibility," *Defense Daily*, October 5, 1999.

Joint Staff, JWCA formulation, working papers, 1995–1996.

Judge Advocate General—*See* U.S. Army Judge Advocate General.

Lewis, Leslie, Roger Allen Brown, John Y. Schrader, *Improving the Army Planning Programming, Budgeting, and Execution System (PPBES): The Programming Phase*, Santa Monica, Calif.: RAND, MR-934-A, 1999

_____, *Improving the Army's Resource Decisionmaking*, Santa Monica, Calif.: RAND, DB-294-A, 2000.

Lewis, Leslie, James A. Coggin, and C. Robert Roll, *The United States Special Operations Command Resource Management Process: An Application of the Strategy-to-Tasks Framework*, Santa Monica, Calif.: RAND, MR-445-A/SOCOM, 1994.

Lewis, Leslie, Zalmay M. Khalilzad, and C. Robert Roll, *New-Concept Development: A Planning Approach for the 21st Century Air Force*, Santa Monica, Calif.: RAND, MR-815-AF, 1996

Lewis, Leslie, Bruce Pirnie, William Williams, and John Y. Schrader, *Defining a Common Planning Framework for the Air Force*, Santa Monica, Calif.: RAND, MR-1006-AF, 1999

Lewis, Leslie, and C. Robert Roll, "Quadrennial Defense Review 2001: Managing Change in the Department of Defense," *National Security Studies Quarterly*, Vol. VI, No. 4, Autumn 2000.

Lewis, Leslie, C. Robert Roll, and John D. Mayer, *Assessing the Structure and Mix of Active and Reserve Forces: Assessment of Policies and Practices for Implementing the Total Force Policy*, Santa Monica, Calif.: RAND, MR-133-OSD, 1992.

Lewis, Leslie, C. Robert Roll, Ronald E. Sortor, and Bernard Rostker, *Organizational Analysis and Resource Management Planning: Annotated Briefing*, Santa Monica, Calif.: RAND, N-3313-A, 1993.

Lewis, Leslie, Harry Thie, Roger Brown, and John Schrader, *Improving the Army Planning, Programming, Budgeting, and Execution System (PPBES): The Planning Phase*, Santa Monica, Calif.: RAND, MR-1133-A, 2000.

Lewis, W. Arthur, *Development Planning: The Essentials of Economic Policy*, New York: Harper and Row, 1966.

Memorandum for JROC Review Board, JWCA Contract Process, CPR 1997, 19 August 1996.

National Defense Panel, *Transitioning to a 21st Century Military*, 1997.

Naval War College, *Resource Allocation: The Formal Process*, Vol. 1, Newport, R.I., August 1998.

Navy—*See* Deparment of the Navy.

NDP—*See* National Defense Panel.

Office of the Chief of Naval Operations, Instruction 5420.108A, September 20, 1997.

QDR 2001 working papers from Joint Staff and OSD, September 2000 to March 2001.

Rice, Donald, SAF, Air Force Reorganization, memorandum, October 2, 1989.

Roll, C. Robert, *Major Issues in Managing the Department of Defense*, Santa Monica, Calif.: RAND, N-2882-RC, 1989.

Schrader, John, Leslie Lewis, Roger Allen Brown, *Quadrennial Defense Review Analysis (QDR) Analysis A Retrospective Look at Joint Staff Participation*, Santa Monica, Calif.: RAND, DB-236-JS, 1999.

Schwabe, William, Leslie Lewis, and John Schrader, *Analytic Architectures for Joint Staff Decision Support Activities: Final Report*, Santa Monica, Calif.: RAND, MR-651-JS, 1996.

Shinseki, GEN Eric, letter of intent, June 23, 1999.

The President's Blue Ribbon Commission on Defense Management, *A Quest for Excellence: Final Report to the President*, June 1986.

Title 10, United States Code.

U.S. Air Force, Policy Directive 10-19, July 1, 1997.

_____, "Air Force Strategic Planning: The Way Ahead," briefing April 9, 1999.

U.S. Army, Army Long-Range Planning System, Army Regulation AR-11-32, January 10, 1989a.

_____, Army Planning, Programming, Budgeting and Execution (PPBES) Process, draft Army Regulation AR-10-1, circa 1989b.

U.S. Army Judge Advocate General, "Implementation of Goldwater-Nichols Legislation," briefing, Falls Church, Va., August 1993.

U.S. Army War College, *How the Army Runs, A Senior Leader Reference Handbook, 1997–1998*, Carlyle Barracks, Penn., 1998.

U.S. Congress, Conference Report 99-824, 99th Congress 2nd Session, September 12, 1986, p. 148.

U.S. Department of Defense, Directive 5134.1, "Under Secretary of Defense for Acquisition, Technology, and Logistics (USD(AT&L))," April 21, 2000.

_____, Directive 5000.1, March 15, 1996.

U.S. General Accounting Office, *Report to the Chairman, Subcommittee on Investigations, Committee on Armed Services, House of Representatives, Acquisition Reform, Military Departments' Response to the Reorganization Act*, Washington D.C., NSIAD-89-70, June 1, 1989.

_____, *Defense Reorganization: Roles of Joint Military Organizations in Resource Allocation*, Washington, D.C., NSIAD-90-76, June 21, 1990.

_____, *Defense Headquarters: Status of Efforts to Reduce Headquarters Personnel*, NSIAD-99-45, February 17, 1999.

VCSA—*See* Vice Chief of Staff of the Army.

Vice Chief of Staff of the Army, Memorandum Through Vice Chief of Staff, Army for Chief of Staff, Army: Phase I, Army Staff Reorganization Decisions, August 1999.

Waterman, Robert, Jr., *Adhocracy: The Power to Change,* New York: W.W. Norton and Company, 1992.

Wickham, John, GEN, outgoing CSA, memorandum to the incoming CSA, May 1987.